# The TEXTILE ARTIST'S STUDIO HANDBOOK

Learn Traditional and Contemporary Techniques for Working with Fiber, Including Weaving, Knitting, Dyeing, Painting, and More

First published in the United States of America in 2012 by
Quarry Books, a member of
Quayside Publishing Group
100 Cummings Center
Suite 406-L
Beverly, Massachusetts 01915-6101
Telephone: (978) 282-9590
Fax: (978) 283-2742
www.quarrybooks.com

10 9 8 7 6 5 4 3 2 1

ISBN: 978-1-59253-777-8

Digital edition published in 2012
eISBN: 978-1-61058-394-7

**Library of Congress Cataloging-in-Publication Data**

Popovic, Visnja.
 The textile artist's studio handbook : traditional and contemporary techniques for working with fiber, including dyeing, painting, and more / Visnja Popovic and Owyn Ruck.
    pages cm
 Summary: "Explore the world of textile arts, one thread at a time! The Textile Artist's Studio Handbook is the only book you need for expanding your repertoire of textile crafting and design techniques. This is the go-to guide for the foundations of design and fabrication, glossary of materials, and classic techniques that include weaving, dyeing, painting, and more! Plus, where else can you get behind-the-scenes access to setting up the best home textile studio for you? Inside, you'll find exploration of basic materials (including fibers, dyes, paints, and other media); visual tutorials for spinning, felting, crochet, weaving, sewing, and quilting; primers for surface decoration techniques such as dyeing, painting, stitching, and screen printing; and patterns and project instructions"-- Provided by publisher.
 ISBN 978-1-59253-777-8 (pbk.)
 1. Textile crafts. I. Ruck, Owyn. II. Title.
 TT699.P66 2012
 746.4--dc23

                                                                      2011050144

Design: Kathie Alexander
Photography: Pauline Shapiro
Cover: All cover images by Pauline Shapiro, except bottom right, istock.com.
Illustrations: Heather Lambert, 153 (top); Lisa Li Hertzi (page 153), (middle and bottom)
Technical editor: Beth Baumgartel

Printed in China

# *The* TEXTILE ARTIST'S STUDIO HANDBOOK

Learn Traditional and Contemporary Techniques for Working with Fiber, Including Weaving, Knitting, Dyeing, Painting, and More

*Owyn Ruck and
Visnja Popovic*

**Quarry Books**
100 Cummings Center, Suite 406L
Beverly, MA 01915

quarrybooks.com • craftside.typepad.com

# Contents

# Foreword by Natalie Chanin

**During one of my very first design-school classes, the professor, who later became my mentor, asked all of us students to close our eyes and relax.** He proceeded to guide us through a short meditation and took us, in our minds of course, to an imaginary studio where he asked us to sit and dream. Strangely enough, the vision I had those many years ago is pretty much the same vision that I have today. Our studio is a safe place. It's the place that we as designers and artists go to do our most important work. It is the place where we are able to breathe.

It has taken me a decade to build my own perfect studio. My company began its odyssey in a three-bedroom brick house on the side of County Road 200; today we work inside an innocuous building that blends seamlessly with the other adjacent metal giants that once served as homes to booming textile production.

However unremarkable the outside of the studio may seem, inside I have managed to carve out a space that undeniably and unmistakably evokes the lifestyle charm of Alabama Chanin. This warehouse is the hub of our operations, yet visitors almost always comment on its homey feel. Its beauty lies in the simplicity and the function of all the pieces that fill it. Everything, from the bales of fabric remnants that create the perfect couch, to the sawhorse-supported tables scattered throughout, serves a purpose and everything is beautiful.

No matter the size and location, textile studios, whether carved out of a room in a home or in a beautiful building by a river, or even in a boxy storage pod, is a place where artists grow and develop. As you spend time working in your space, you will discover a myriad of creative ways to utilize its unique features. Over the years, the artisan in me has grown from textile designer, to fashion designer, to author, and my studio has grown with me. Had I taken a snapshot of my studio while working on each of my books, each image would be wildly different, but perfectly suited to my mood and style at that time.

I have gone through periods when cluttered inspiration boards and mountains of thumbtacks seemed imperative to my process; other times, only clean lines and white walls have been able to quiet my mind and allow me to streamline my thoughts. It is essential to invest enough time to create an environment that serves you, to carve out a space that works, and to continually reevaluate your space and your dreams. The benefits of doing so will astound you. The book that you hold in your hand is a lovely place to start.

**ALABAMA CHANIN** is a lifestyle company that creates products for the individual and the home, focusing on slow design and sustainability. www.alabamachanin.com

**NATALIE CHANIN** is the designer behind Alabama Chanin and the author of three books: *Alabama Stitch Book* (STCraft - February, 2008), *Alabama Studio Style* (STCraft - March, 2010) and the upcoming *Alabama Studio Design* (STCraft - 2012).

# Introduction

**Take a minute to observe your surroundings.** What covers your windows? What do you love about that cozy couch you're sitting on? Do you know how your shirt was screen printed, or how your rug was woven? Textiles encompass a huge part of our world, but many of us have no idea about the journey that fibers take to become the products that you own and wear and enjoy.

Within all of us there is a desire and a talent to create, whether it is ideas, music, or physical objects. The ability to create with your own hands eases the mind, soothes the soul, and supports a sense of self-sufficiency. If you've ever had the slight desire to dive into the world of textiles or envisioned the space in which you could do so, the book you hold in your hands is the perfect starting point.

To us, it's an exciting time for textiles. Our management of the Textile Arts Center in New York City has given us a unique perspective on the prevailing attitude towards textiles. While fiber arts and crafts enjoyed a resurgence of popularity in the 1960s and '70s sparking a wide debate on arts versus crafts, the emerging interest in textiles is something entirely different. Once seen as more practical in application, the design and creation of textiles is now achieving recognition as an art form. With the success of DIY (think Etsy, Handmade Nation), the growth in the sustainable fashion movement, and the increasing use of textile media among fine artists, the descriptions of textile design and textile artists have changed from stodgy, crafty, and old to useful, beautiful, and even hip. Today, it seems that nothing is cooler than being able to say you made it yourself.

While the joy of creating is extremely important and something we always want to foster, we also have another goal, and that is education. As university students, we started the Textile Arts Center with a love and understanding of textiles and their importance, as well as a desire to preserve hand-craft techniques that were becoming forgotten. For us, preservation relies on education.

At the Center, we've met people of all ages, races, economic backgrounds, and career paths, all with their own reason for wanting to learn about textiles. We have often been shocked. How could there be a print designer who had never screen printed before? How could a designer study in fashion school and never touch a loom? As time passes, we are more motivated than ever about our mission to educate people about textiles, not just their importance or history, but the fundamental processes that lead to great design.

Our physical space at the Textile Arts Center is home to classes, workshops, and events in all forms of textile media. So, as authors we wanted to address a wide range of fiber media in this book as well. We learned all of the fabulous ways to create textiles by diving in and setting up a giant studio, and we want to share our experiences.

While there will always be some processes that draw you more than others, some fibers that you can't wait to work with, and beautiful environments that inspire you, there will also be many resources and books on your journey to help you explore textile media. Our wish is to provide you with a foundation upon which to grow. It is our hope that you will feel inspired to set up your own studio, get your hands dirty, and learn through the exploration and understanding of the fundamental principles of textiles.

— Owyn Ruck and Visnja Popovic,
Textile Arts Center

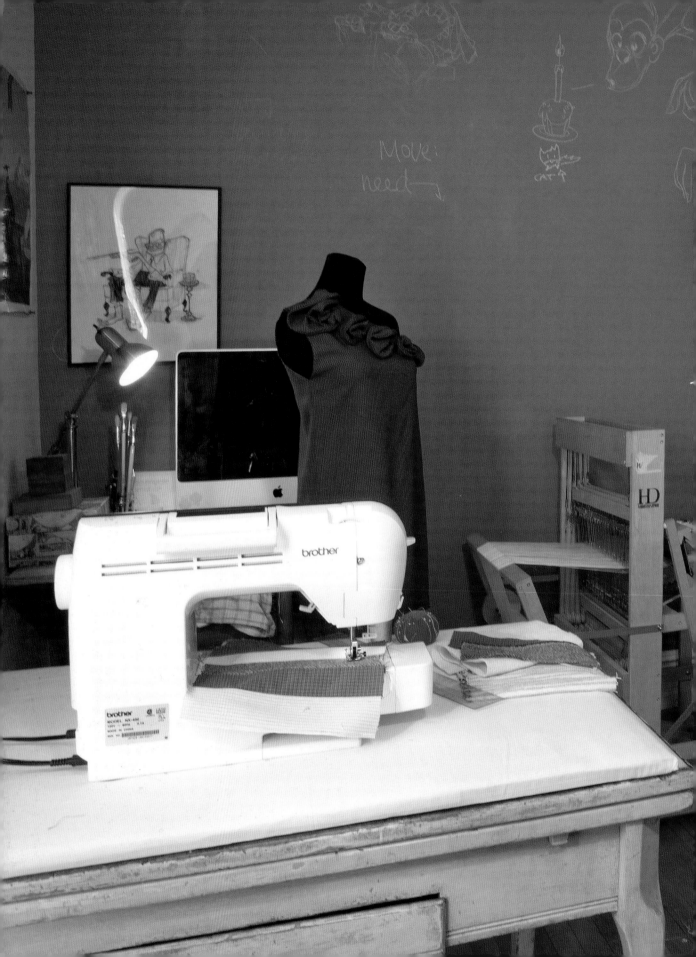

# Building a Home
# Textile Studio

While the size, shape, and configuration of your home textile studio may change over time, understanding the foundational needs is the first step in creating a successful workspace. The first part of this book lays the groundwork for a textile studio that allows for growth in both space and the ability to expand the type of textile media techniques you explore.

# Planning the Layout

**Fabric and fiber play as large a part in everyday life as they do in art and art history.** One might think that with the advancements in technology, we would have lost our taste for the tactile arts, but nothing could be further from the truth. Sewing, knitting, quilting, and other fiber arts have come to the foreground in a big way in recent years and have attracted a whole new generation of enthusiasts. Handmade products have wide appeal among makers and consumers alike. Buying, using, and making handmade products supports local designers and craftspeople, offers a creative outlet, and is better for the environment than buying mass-produced items.

If you are considering setting up a designated workspace for your textile projects, it probably means that you are tired of working out of your living room on small knitting projects and dyeing yarns in your cooking pots or bathtub. Whether you just want more space for a well-loved hobby or want to turn it into a moneymaking business, setting up a textile studio requires a little thought and planning. This chapter will help you to set up your studio so that you can comfortably and efficiently explore your creativity through the rich world of textiles.

While a beautiful and inspirational space is important to your work, your primary concern should be utility. Ample storage ensures organization and accessibility.

## Workspace Requirements

Consider each of the following areas of textile media carefully to ensure that you choose the best setup for the types of media you want to explore. A studio is a large investment, and though we are certain it will bring you great joy, satisfaction, and exploration opportunities, you'll want to consider how much space you have, access to certain resources, and how much money you are willing to spend.

### Shopping List for Building Your Studio

Refer to this checklist when planning your studio space:

- Versatile worktable(s)
- Chair, bench, or stool
- Variety of yarns (content, color, weight)
- Cubbies and bins for storage in both wet and dry areas
- Dyes and dye pots kept close to your wet area
- Loom and weaving tools
- Spindle and spinning supplies
- Sewing machine and sewing supplies
- Dress form and sewing notions
- Variety of fabrics, especially muslin
- Light box for screen printing in a dark area
- Printing screens and other printing tools for block printing
- Safety equipment
- Full-spectrum work lamps

**TOP** A floor loom is a great asset in a textile studio. Creating your own fabric from beginning to end is highly rewarding. Shown here is an 8-harness, 10-treadle, 48" (1.2 m) Harrisville floor loom.

## Weaving

Weaving requires ample floor space, as well as storage for the many tools and gadgets you will use. You'll also use lots of yarn, so dry storage that is safe from pests is important.

If you would like to weave, a loom is your most important investment. There are various types of looms to suit your budget and available space. No matter the size, a standard floor loom will take up the most space and be most expensive. If you are just getting interested in weaving, you may opt for a smaller table loom or less bulky tapestry, or peg loom (see chapter 5).

Here are some things to consider about setting up a weaving studio:

- Do I have enough room for a floor loom? A standard 36" (91.4 cm) floor loom can take up to 45–50 square feet (4.2–4.6 square meters) of space including the space needed to move around the loom to dress it and weave. Many modern looms fold up quite nicely, but folding can be cumbersome and cause problems with the project on the loom. If this amount of floor space does not seem reasonable for your available space, consider starting with a smaller table or rigid heddle loom.

- What kind of storage will I need for easy organization? You'll want both dry storage and ways in which to organize tools. Small drawers or bins that stack work well. Weaving requires storing many small items, but also some larger items like a warping board and bobbin winder. The warping board can be hung on a wall, and the bobbin winder can attach to the top of a table.

- Do I have space to store cones of yarn? Yarn is the material you'll use most in weaving, and you'll want to buy a variety of yarns, many of which will be held on cones (versus a skein, or ball). Invest in a variety of yarn weights, fiber contents, and colors so that you can experiment with the effects of different yarns before beginning your projects.

## Needle Arts

Needle arts such as sewing, embroidery, felting, knitting, and crochet require storage space and a high level of organization. One needle is not the same as another, and a sewing machine needle will not be useful when you are ready to try some hand embroidery. Although there are a lot of small tools and materials to organize and store, the space you need to knit, crochet, spin yarn, or embroider is very little—a comfortable place to sit and the few tools and materials you need per project and you are set.

Sewing does require quite a bit of room, especially table space for your sewing machine and cutting out patterns and/or fabric. It is important to be able to spread out while you are working. You will also need room for an iron and ironing board.

Felting, like sewing, has a few more requirements. For wet felting, you will need a water source (though does not have to be nearby) and ample table space for water bins and the felting practice itself. Of course, you can always cover a table with a waterproof tarp. Dry felting is simpler. You'll need table space and the necessary materials for your specific projects.

Here are the main ideas you should consider if you want to concentrate on needle arts:

- Will I have enough room for an amply sized table? Expansive projects might require that you spread out on the floor; however, a 6' x 3' (1.8 x 0.9 m) table should be large enough for most projects.

- Can I create a versatile tabletop myself? For many needle arts projects, a padded tabletop comes in handy. We show you how to make one on page 26.

- Where will I sit for long periods of time? Make sure you have a comfortable sitting arrangement to avoid backache.

- Where will I store my things? Practically all needle art supplies, including tools and materials, should be stored in a dry place. Plastic bins and bags are great for roving, while a spool stand is perfect for holding sewing threads.

# Screen and Block Printing

Two of the most common printing methods used in home textile studios are block printing and screen printing. Block printing doesn't require very much special equipment, or very much space. Screen printing is a bit more involved and requires space, water, and a few basic supplies. Screen printing, like weaving, has equipment choices based on the type of work you hope to create. Equipment can range from a professional-grade vacuum-sealed exposure unit to humbler home-built alternatives (page 114). Doing it yourself with home-built supplies may save money, but the space requirements will be about the same.

Consider the following:

- Do I have space to make a darkroom? If you are screen printing and using photo emulsion, you will need a dark area. The chemicals used for this kind of stencil are light sensitive, so the chemicals and the exposure screens need to be stored in the dark.

- What will I use to burn a screen? This is an important budgetary consideration. A fancy vacuum-sealed exposure unit works incredibly fast and well, but is expensive. Visit a local print shop to see what their fees are for exposing screens. Another option is to make an exposure unit yourself. You can find the materials you need at a hardware store and make it to the size that best fits your studio. Although it is not nearly as fast or efficient, the cost is minimal. See page 114 for a tutorial on how to make an exposure light box.

- Do I have access to a water source? A water source is a definite need so you can clean your screens thoroughly between printing colors or finished layers. A regular garden or sink hose works well, but an outside source is best if you don't have a dedicated sink or washout booth so that ink does not get on your kitchen or bathroom goods. If you need to remove a stencil from a screen (a.k.a. "reclaiming a screen"), you will need access to a power washer. Block printing and the use of hand-cut stencils still require a water source, but no special equipment.

- Do I have a good size, padded table space? Printing can require considerable space depending on what you are creating. If you are printing small tea towels, tote bags, or T-shirts, a small space is adequate. However, if you are interested in printing larger pieces, you will want enough table space to print your repeat designs. Printing on paper or one-off T-shirts and tote bags does not need a padded surface, but printing on yardage does. A padded surface allows you to pin the fabric in place and provides some buoyancy for the printing process. See page 26 for making a padded tabletop.

- Where can I store inks and pigments? Any kind of dark cabinet works as long as it is removed from the water source. You can store pots and utensils near a wet area, but inks, dyes, pigments, and chemicals should be kept away from water. Labeling cabinets on the outside is helpful so you can easily differentiate between dyes, inks, and chemicals.

Screen printing, which can be done several ways depending on your needs, budget, and space, will always need a source of water.

Natural dyes are beautiful to have around, even as raw materials. You can use clear plastic or glass jars with tight lids to display them as well as for storage.

## DYEING

Dyeing, including natural dyeing, which is explored in chapter 9, requires a water-friendly workspace, such as your kitchen or bathroom; however, a water source dedicated to your studio is ideal. It's difficult to keep your kitchen pots and utensils separate from your dye equipment when you work in your kitchen. If you must work from your kitchen or bathroom, we suggest using storage in your studio area for the dyes, pots, tools, etc. Shown here are natural dye materials that are kept in sealed glass jars and can be stored with dye pots, hot plates, measuring tools, and mordants. If you do use your kitchen utensils, be sure to clean them thoroughly to remove all chemicals.

The dye lab is the area of the studio used for dyeing, and as the name suggests, it requires a source of water, as well as heat, ventilation, and storage for chemicals. The heat source, necessary for making dye baths and steam-setting dyes, can be your kitchen stove, or it can be simple hot plates or Bunsen burners, which are easy to store and transport. Ventilation is important and can be tricky, but if you are using nontoxic natural and synthetic dyes, you can get away with a window draft system. You should not practice any kind of dyeing in a room that has no windows. Some dyes are degraded by direct light, so storage is an important consideration. A screen-printing darkroom can double as storage for textiles and dyes that need to be protected from natural light.

Here are the major considerations for creating a dye lab:

- Do I have a place to work that is close to a water and heat source? A water source is vital to dyeing; otherwise, you cannot create a dye bath. Likewise, some dyes cannot be used without heat. It is ideal to have your water and heat source in the space in which you are dyeing; however, if your kitchen is the best place, simply take care to clean thoroughly.

- Do I have a place to work in with proper ventilation? Windows are a must in a dyeing space. A fancy ventilation system is not necessary because you should only be using nontoxic dyes. Chemicals can be harmful, so avoid contact as a precaution.

- Do I have a place to store dyes and pigments in a dry, dark place that is separate from yarn and fabric storage? You won't want dyes, inks, or pigments to accidentally get on any of your fiber materials.

- Do I have access to a washer/dryer or large sink for rinsing as well as a place for line drying? Water source is necessary for rinsing fibers and fabrics. A clothes washer and dryer are not necessary, but they are nice to have close by. A large sink is sufficient for rinsing and washing fabrics, and a laundry line or drying rack will also do the trick.

*See chapter 7 for more information.*

If you don't like the look of LED light-ing, install a variety of lights. Here are florescent and halogen lights, which will provide a neutral light source.

## The Raw Space

Now that you have thought about the array of tech-niques you can practice in a textile studio, there are a few basic space issues to consider. Keep the follow-ing in mind:

- The floor and surfaces should be completely clean-able. (As a fiber lover, you must love rugs and drap-ery, but in a studio they are not a good idea.)

- You will need a sufficient amount of electricity. The outlets should be well distributed. Having many will allow for unhindered movement and avoid acci-dents. Outlets can be on walls, on floors, or retract-able from the ceiling.

- North-facing natural light is ideal because it is neu-tral in the color spectrum. Colors are most true in neutral light. You will also need to have plenty of artificial light—LED "Daylight" bulbs are best. In-stalling blinds or shades will be important. Win-dows can function as a simple ventilation system.

- You don't need a sink in your main area, but con-sider installing a utility or slop sink somewhere near by, perhaps in a bathroom. Plastic utility sinks are cheap, but dyes might stain them. Stainless steel sinks are easier to maintain, but pricier. Some mate-rials and chemicals shouldn't be mixed in everyday dishes even if they are nontoxic, so invest in a set of dishes and reserve it for studio use only.

 **Use Full Spectrum Lighting**

Full-spectrum is incandescent or fluorescent light measuring more than 5500K (degrees Kelvin) and 91CRI (Color Rendering Index), meaning that it closely matches sunlight. This gives you bright, non-glare light that blends with daylight and offers good color rendition.

## COMPONENTS OF A VERSATILE STUDIO

There are four very basic components that are necessary for most textile design: the worktable, a heat source, water source/wet area, and dry/dark areas. Each component serves many different media.

**The Work Table**  You will need table space for just about every type of project, so make sure to select a table that is versatile. It should be sturdy and large for both convenience and safety, but should optimize the space it takes up by using the underside for storage with drawers or vertical slots for screens. Transform the table with a removable padded top that can be stored when not in use. A hard surface is good for some things, but a padded top is essential for printing on fabric and helpful when sewing garments. Instructions for making a simple padded table topper are at the end of this chapter. If you are on a tight budget, your dining room table will work well, but you might disturb other parts of your life.

 **TIP**  **The Keys to Storage**

Consider all your workspaces as possible space for storage. Organization within your storage areas is key, keeping tools and materials less cluttered and easier to find. Use small bins or drawers, zipper lock plastic bags, or drawer separators to make space for the various things you'll need. You can find some lovely, more expensive storage choices, or a trip to a dollar store could prove a source of inexpensive, yet functional storage items.

**TOP**  The table shown here can be completely modified with a removable padded table top, vertical slots for screen storage, and drawers for storing fabric and other materials.

**MIDDLE**  A work table that works best for your lifestyle will work best for your studio. It's fine if you will need to use your dining table because you can make a padded table topper to protect it. The table topper also makes it easy for you to work anywhere.

**LEFT**  Store your yarn cones on yarn trees to make them accessible from all sides. The yarn trees keep yarns from getting dusty or moth-eaten and if you put them on wheels, they are completely mobile.

# Which Studio Components Will You Need?

This chart shows you the components to consider based on the textile media you plan to explore.

| AREA | Felting | Dyeing | Screen + Block Printing | Knitting, Crochet, Spinning | Embroidery, Sewing, Quilting | Weaving |
|---|---|---|---|---|---|---|
| Versatile Work Table | X | X Larger space (padded) | X Larger space (padded) | X Smaller space (not padded) | X Larger space (padded) | NO |
| Wet Area/ Water Source | X (for wet felting) | X | X (plus access to a hose) | NO | NO | NO |
| Heat source | X | X (especially for natural dyeing) | X (if printing with dyes) | NO | NO | NO |
| Dry, Dark Storage | NO | Dyes, pigments, chemicals, dye tools, pots | Coated screen, inks, pigments, chemicals | NO (unless you have fibers that need to be UV protected over long periods of time) | NO (unless you have fibers that need to be UV protected over long periods of time) | NO |
| Dry Storage | For roving, small tools and needles | Fabrics, fiber, and yarns for dyeing | Fabrics for printing | Threads, small tools | Sewing machine, threads, fabrics, patterns/ pattern paper | Yarn cones, weaving tools, newsprint |
| Additional Considerations | Drying rack | Drying rack | Drying Rack | Comfortable seating | Floor space to spread if table space is too small | Considerable floor space needed for a standard floor loom |

**Heat Source** A heat source, such as a stovetop, is vital for several textile processes, especially dyeing. It is mostly used for heating water, creating dye baths, steaming and finishing fabric, heating wax for batik, and shrinking wool. You can choose to use your kitchen gas range or several hot plates. Sometimes, the processes that require heat take a lot of time. If you don't want to tie up your kitchen area, hot plates work just as well. Single or double-sized hot plates store very easily. You should never leave them unattended.

**Water Source and Wet Area** A water source is important for dyeing, felting, and screen printing, but it doesn't necessarily have to be in the studio space. A bathroom sink or bathtub will work just fine; just be sure to clean thoroughly.

If you can install a water source within your studio, a utility sink with both hot and cold water is ideal. A small counter space directly next to it and storage either above or below makes the area very work-friendly.

Other helpful equipment, if space and money allow, are a washer and dryer dedicated to washing and finishing your newly created fabrics. You can also hook up a power washer and washout booth for screen printing to this same water source, as long as they are far from the dry areas. Again, consider the media you are most interested in exploring and plan the space accordingly. If you are primarily interested in weaving or sewing, you don't need a wet space or water source, but if dyeing seems particularly intriguing, be sure there is a sink close by or inside your studio space.

Though this antique spinning wheel is missing parts, keeping such beautiful, historically rich tools around your workspace may inspire you. And you can often fix old tools and machines and bring them back to life—often for a lower cost than buying something new.

**Dry and Dark Areas** A dry area is just as important as a wet area. Use your dry areas for storage, needlework, spinning, sewing, and anything that doesn't require water. Yarns, fibers, and fabric should remain dry until you are using them for wet processes, such as dyeing. The separation of wet and dry areas is very important. It can be frustrating to have your fabric ruined by a spot of ink or a drop of dye bath that was mistakenly left on a table!

In addition to wet/dry areas, consider that certain processes, such as exposing screens for printing, are light sensitive. So if you plan to screen print and store dyes and pigments that are light sensitive, you'll need dark areas in addition to your illuminated workspace. If you do not have a windowless bathroom, closet, or dedicated space, you can use blackout shades on your windows or work at night. Regardless of the type of dark space, install red or yellow safelights.

 **Get New Pots**

Make sure you have a separate set of pots or containers to hold your dyes and pigments. You don't want to use the tools from your living space for your studio work; you'll need different items for each!

# Organization, Safety, and Conservation

Organization is key to productivity and safety. Here are some things to keep in mind when setting up the studio and organizing your materials and equipment.

**Labeling:** No matter how much money you spend on supplies, if you don't know where they are, you may as well not have them! Different storage systems work for different people. Make your labels large and clear. Affix labels to all drawers, cabinets, bins, and such. All chemicals, including dyes, inks, fixatives, and mordants, must be clearly labeled and kept in a dedicated area.

**Storage:** Cubbies, drawers, or small containers are essential for differentiating between various tools and materials (including needles, small weaving accessories, etc.). Be realistic about your needs and how they may change as your hobby, art, or business grows. Investing in larger storage furniture than you first need will allow you to expand without repeatedly having to graduate to larger models. You do not need to run out and buy anything special, but your storage system needs to work for you and the level of organization you desire. Some people prefer more compartmentalization than others. You can find small baskets or plastic bins at dollar stores, or even small and large drawer units at places like IKEA. For yarns and fabric, it is best to use plastic to keep pests out. For small tools, drawer dividers or small boxes and baskets work well.

**Sort by Fiber:** Keep yarns separated by fiber content. Wool reacts differently than cotton. You don't want to mix up these materials unless you don't mind your sweater turning into an art piece the first time you wash it! Balls and skeins should be kept in sealable plastic bins or drawers to keep out dust, moisture, and moths. Thread cones can be stored on shelves but are most accessible on a rotating yarn tree or on a peg board on the wall, which also helps with pest management because of the constant movement. If unlabeled fibers get mixed, you can conduct a "burn test" to help differentiate the fibers (page 40).

**ABOVE** Clearly labeled tools are more likely to be used and put back where they belong.

**BELOW** Taking the time to keep your materials neat and organized will save you time and energy. This sewing table includes drawers, which are very helpful.

# Protecting Your Work: Basic Textile Conservation

Textile conservation is a broad field of study and research, with focus on the preservation of textile and fiber heritage, including conservation treatment procedures, preventive measures, and the study of the history, materials, and techniques.

We associate textile conservation with museum and gallery practices, but traditionally textiles have been preserved in a domestic environment through the simple acts of mending and washing. Most of the textiles in our daily lives don't fall under the heritage category, but hopefully one day your artwork might! Although textile conservation diagnostics and treatments should be left to professional conservators and setting up your studio with museum conditions would not only be complicated but expensive, your artwork and materials will definitely benefit from you knowing the very basic textile conservation principles.

One of the most important principles of textile conservation is preventive conservation, which considers and monitors all the factors that can lead to the degradation of textiles. Factors include environmental conditions (light, temperature, relative humidity), control of insects and mold, and storage conditions.

Here's a bit more on how you can use basic textile conservation techniques in your own studio.

## ENVIRONMENTAL CONDITIONS

Light, temperature, and relative humidity are all factors that effect the degradation of textiles.

**Lighting**  The right light is extremely important while working on textiles; it allows better perception of color and makes a more comfortable working environment for the artist. However, most of the time, the optimum light conditions for the artist aren't necessarily the optimum conditions for the preservation of textile artwork. Fibers and dyes are light sensitive and continuous exposure, especially to ultra violet radiation (UV), will initiate and/or enhance their degradation process. Dyes, natural and synthetic, are especially sensitive, and overexposure to light might lead to fad-

Goggles, gloves, dust masks, and aprons must be readily available.

**Inventory:** Whether you are creating textiles for yourself or for others, as a hobby or as a business, you should maintain an inventory of your materials indicting where you bought them. This will help keep you organized and be helpful when you are ordering materials. You'll quickly discover favorite sources for materials, so an inventory system will help you remember the places you do and don't like to order from.

**Safety:** Always keep safety gear close at hand—this way, you are more likely to use it. Goggles, gloves, dust masks, and aprons are essential in a textile studio. If your budget allows, consider purchasing an eye washer that can be attached to your faucet if you have a wet area in your studio.

ing or alteration of the colors, and fibers over time can become brittle.

UV radiation is present in natural daylight and most fluorescent lighting; however, you can take some steps to minimize the effect of light on the degradation of your textiles.

1. Line your windows with UV blocking materials or replace the window glass with UV-blocking glass.

2. Keep your blinds down whenever you're not working in the studio.

3. Choose light bulbs with a UV filter.

Remember that the effect of light is cumulative and four months of intense exposure to light is equivalent to several years of moderate exposure. Keep this in mind whenever you're sending your artwork to an exhibition (four months is generally the maximum recommended display time) and try to store your textiles in a dark place whenever you're not working on or displaying them.

## Relative Humidity and Temperature

High temperatures and humidity accelerate the deterioration of fibers and dyes, and are also the most favorable conditions for the development of mold, mildew, and insects. Temperature and relative humidity conditions should be kept at values between 65–70°F (18–21°C) and 50–55 percent humidity. Avoid drastic fluctuations of temperature and humidity, as they can be very stressful for the fibers and textile structures and can lead to damage. Air-conditioning and central heating will keep the studio temperature constant; maintain the ideal humidity with humidifiers or dehumidifiers. Be sure to check your space for possible leaks or water infiltration, especially in places that aren't readily accessible.

## Pests

There are many kinds of pests that threaten textiles, the most common being moths, carpet beetles, silverfish, and rodents. Moths and carpet beetles prefer protein fibers, such as wool and silk, while silverfish prefer cellulose-based fibers (see page 31).

The key word here is prevention, because once invaders settle in, it is very hard to get rid of them. The best way to prevent pest damage is by denying the pests a safe place to live in the first place. Once again, temperature and humidity are very important, as most of pests favor warm, humid environments. It is also very important to keep your place clean and organized. Needless to say, food should be kept out of the studio and storage areas.

It is also important to learn to recognize your enemy, especially because they can assume different forms over their life cycles. Become familiar with the most common textile-loving insects and do routine inspections of your space, artwork, and materials. Buy insect glue traps and place them in strategic places, even if you never notice any sign of infestation. They will help you monitor the pest situation in your studio and will provide the first signs of alert in case of infestation.

One very common way of introducing pests into your studio is through your materials. We all love a bargain, and yard, warehouse, or online auction sales offer numerous opportunities to buy affordable materials. Because eye inspections sometimes might not be enough, all the materials sourced from "unknown" suppliers should be kept in quarantine before entering your studio space. Place suspicious yarn or fabric in a zipper lock plastic bag and leave it in the freezer for a few days to kill any active infestation, including eggs.

## STORAGE

All storing and packing materials should be archival to ensure that the materials in contact with the textile will not significantly contribute to their degradation. Cardboard tubes, boxes, and paper used to store textiles should be acid free because an acidic environment will accelerate the degradation of fibers. For the same reason, textiles should not be stored on wooden shelves or in wooden cabinets or boxes since wood constantly releases acids. If you can't avoid using wooden storage, seal the wood first and use acid-free paper as a barrier between the wood and the textile. Plexiglas, glass, and stainless steel storage options are the most recommended.

Textiles should be stored flat to minimize any tension to the structures or fibers. However, this solution isn't very space friendly, so if you need to constrain your storage space, the best option is to roll your textiles on a tube, with layers of acid free paper between the textiles. The roll should be covered with cotton muslin to protect the textiles from light and dust. This last storage option doesn't work for three-dimensional textiles, such as garments. Garments and other three-dimensional textiles can be hung on hangers padded with cotton batting to minimize tension and protected with a muslin cover. If the textile is too heavy for hanging and too dimensional for rolling, store it in a large box, with tissue paper used as padding for any folds, volume, or creases.

Your storage area should follow the same guidelines for light, temperature, relative humidity, and pest management as mentioned previously.

# How to Make a Padded Table Topper

When you want to adapt your hard-surface worktable for working with fabric, consider making a sturdy removable padded table topper. The padded surface is more suitable than a hard surface for fabric printing, sewing, quilting, and even some felting. Here is a tutorial on how to get started.

## TOOLS

- Staple gun
- Scissors or rotary cutter
- Yardstick or ruler
- Washing machine and dryer
- Optional: sand paper

## MATERIALS

- 1" (2.5 cm) thick ply-wood cut to desired size (see step 1)
- Cotton or synthetic batting (2" [5.1 cm] longer and wider than plywood)
- Thick cotton canvas fabric (12" [30.5 cm] longer and wider than plywood)

## INSTRUCTIONS

1. Measure the size of the table that the padded top will rest on. Decide whether you want to provide more surface area than the table below or if you want it to be the same size. We recommend adding about 6" (15.2 cm) to each side of the table measurements.

2. Order a sheet of plywood from your local hardware store, cut to the desired size.

3. Because the back of the padded table topper won't be completely covered by fabric, you can sand and finish the wood to give extra protection to the existing table top. This is optional.

4. Prep your canvas by washing and drying it on a normal setting in your washing machine and dryer. Iron the dry canvas so that it is wrinkle free.

5. Cut the canvas so it extends 6 inches (15.2 cm) beyond the plywood on all sides. You might have to sew two pieces of canvas together.

6. Cut two separate layers of batting or fold the batting in half depending on the desired size of the batting. The batting can be the same size as the piece of plywood, or you can add 1 inch (2.5 cm) on each side, so that it folds over the edges of the wood, making more comfortable sides.

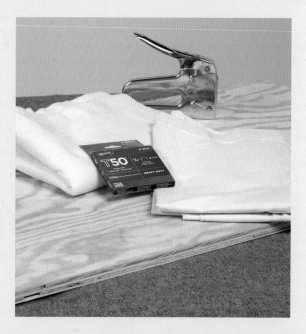

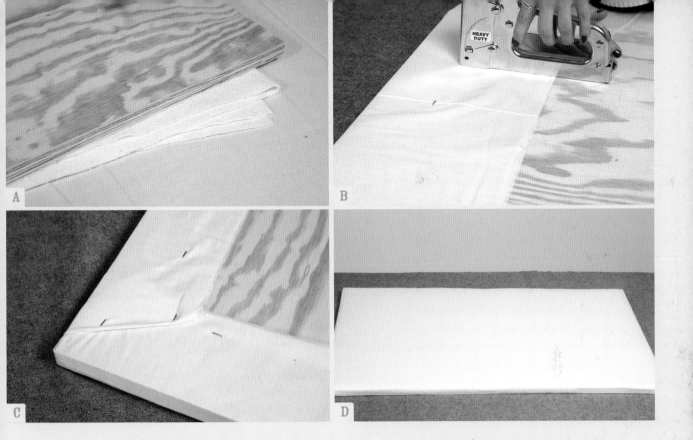

7. Lay out the fabric with the right side down on a large, flat surface. Place the two layers of batting in the center of the fabric. Carefully place the plywood directly on top of the batting. **[A]**

8. With the help of another person, stretch and staple the fabric to the back of the plywood. Start at one end and staple the fabric into the wood every 5 inches (12.7 cm). You can inset the staples fairly close to the edge of the wood. **[B]**

9. Pull the fabric from the opposite side so it is taut over the batting and staple it in place. Once the two opposite ends are stapled, repeat the process on the remaining two sides. Trim the fabric at the corners and fold it neatly before stapling.

10. After you've stapled all the sides, trim away any excess fabric fairly close to the staples. **[C]** Make sure that the fabric is evenly taut.

11. Center the table topper over your table and get to work! **[D]**

Another way to create a padded table topper is to cover a table that you already own. Following the packaging instructions, install grommets evenly around the edge of the prepared fabric. Create a batting "bed" by cutting two layers of batting the same size as the table topper and then sew a square of muslin (or broadcloth) to cover the batting or simply sew all the edges of the batting layers together so that they fold up neatly for storage. Position the batting bed on the table and lay the cover over it. Use bungee cords to connect the grommets on the underside of the table from opposing ends.

# Fiber Basics

**All fabrics, prior to construction, come from fibers.** Fiber is a general term for thread, yarn, or filaments—the fundamental core of fabric content. It is important to remember that fibers are where textile art begins.

The history of fibers goes as far back as recorded human history. Natural fibers such as sheep wool, hemp, and linen have been used for more than 5,000 years, while man-made fibers date as far back as the nineteenth century. Needless to say, the list of fibers, their uses, and chemical make up, is long. Here is a brief explanation of the difference between the basic natural and man-made fibers. This basic understanding will be helpful in selecting fibers and fabrics for your textile studio and for future projects.

Fiber can come in many forms, from many sources, and can create numerous outcomes for your textile work. Shown are cones of both synthetic and natural fiber yarns on yarn trees, which are great organizers. Cones are usually used for weaving and machine knitting.

Natural fibers and fabrics are very desirable and have great qualities. They are often mimicked very well by synthetic fibers.

## Natural Fibers

Natural fibers are those that occur in nature. They come from animals (protein) or plants (cellulose) and require no human intervention in their creation, only in their harvesting. Wool, cotton, silk, and linen are among the most popular natural fibers and are harvested in many places around the world. Though the average person probably won't harvest fiber from the environment, it's very interesting for everyone to understand where the yarns and fibers they use come from. Fiber knowledge will give you a better understanding of the materials you are working with, making you better able to anticipate their behavior. Dyeing, for example, and getting the desired colors and effects depends greatly on the fiber being dyed.

You can purchase a wide array of natural fibers at most yarn shops, and you can order them online. Before purchasing anything for your studio, learn a bit about the basic characteristics of the all fibers, including how they react to heat, water, and chemicals. Here are some basic properties you should know:

- Hot water will cause cotton to shrink. Knit cotton will generally shrink evenly, while woven cottons will shrink more along the warp threads.

- Hot water and friction will felt your wool and other protein-based fibers (and shrink them significantly).

- Silk is very delicate, so wash it gently and avoid using chemicals on it.

- Linen is a beautiful and simple fiber to work with; it is sturdy for sewing, a great strong warp yarn for weaving, and accepts dye very well.

- Linen can sometimes require special treatment. Don't dry it in a dryer and take care not to wring out water too harshly before line drying. Linen also attracts mildew more than other natural fibers, so don't store it until it has dried fully, especially in plastic.

- Hemp fabric and yarn is extremely durable and soft. It is the only natural fiber that is stronger wet than dry, so washing hemp is not harmful. Like cotton, hemp fabric gets much softer over time.

## Protein Fibers

Animals produce protein fibers; amino acids condense to create repeating polymer units, forming fibers of varying elasticity, strength, and resiliency. While there are many different protein fibers, they are broken down into two major classes: keratin and secreted.

**Keratin Fibers** Keratin fibers include hair, fur, and wool. Most commonly we think of sheep, alpaca, camels, and rabbits as the sources of keratin fibers, but even horse, cat, dog, and human hair have been used to create yarn. Mink or beaver fur is often blended with wool to create luxury material. The commonality among keratin fibers is that they must be spun or felted in order to use them as yarn for the creation of fabric.

Individual keratin strands are called "staples," which vary in length depending on the animal. A longer staple generally produces a stronger spun yarn, whereas shorter staple fibers create weaker spun yarn and are often used for felting (see chapter 3), which means that they don't have to go through the process of becoming yarn. In wool production, factors such as staple length, the crimp in the fiber, and the amount of vegetable matter found in the fleece determine quality.

**Secreted Fibers** Secreted fibers come from insects such as silk worms, mites, and spiders and are in the form of a continuous thread (no spinning required). The ectodermic glands of these animals allow them to create silk fibers. The composition of protein sequences varies greatly in each species and therefore in the type of silk they produce. Spiders, for example, produce a variety of different silk filaments, all with different properties, making the web they spin better suited to their environment and subsequently to capturing prey, protecting eggs, and mobility. Almost all the secreted fibers used in textile production come from silk worms, but spiders are amazing spinners!

 **Ethics of Silk**

When we think of silk, we usually think of the silkworm (*Bombyx mori*). The silkworm develops from a larva to a moth/butterfly, creating a secreted fiber that forms a tightly wrapped cocoon, which hardens upon exposure to air. Generally, the larva emerges from the cocoon fully morphed, leaving behind the broken cocoon, which is no longer one continuous thread. In silk production, cocoons are boiled, killing the newly morphed insect before it can break the cocoon so the thread can be harvested in one continuous silk thread.

In recent years, the ethics of this method have been under scrutiny. "Peace silk" refers to silk that has been extracted without harming the insect, allowing it to complete its natural life cycle. The fiber, though broken, is then spun in the same way as other thread or yarn.

## CELLULOSE FIBERS

Cellulose fibers are found in the leaves, stems (bast), and seed hairs of some plants and vegetation. One popular cellulose fiber is cotton, a prime example of a fiber found in a plant seed. A cotton seedpod contains several seeds, each of which can grow about 20,000 fibers. Other, lesser-known plant-seed fibers include coir, which comes from the husk of coconuts and is known for its durability, and kopak, from the Java tree. Kopak is used to fill lifejackets and as pillow stuffing, and it is known for its buoyancy.

Other well-known cellulose fibers, such as flax (linen), ramie, hemp, and jute, come from the stem, or bast, of the plant. These fibers are part of the integrity and strength of the plant, running lengthwise up the stem.

Cellulose fibers that come from the leaves of certain plants include sisal, abaca, and pina. These fibers are used when strength and durability is most important, such as in the production of rope, cord, and floormats.

 **Considering Hemp**

Hemp was one of the first natural fibers to be used by humans. Today, it is one of the most sustainable fiber plants because it grows extremely fast with little water. Hemp fibers are very strong and soft and are often used in the textile and fashion industries. However, some countries such as the United States have banned the growth of hemp plants, despite the plants sustainability as a resource, because of its relationship to marijuana. Though hemp fibers and marijuana can be harvested from the same plant, there have been strains of hemp plants developed to contain very low levels of tetrahydrocannabinol, which is the chemical that creates the "high." Perhaps at some point, it will be possible to regulate the growth of hemp plants so that the sustainability of the species can be used to its full potential.

## Processes for Extracting Plant Fibers

There are several processes used to extract fibers from plants. While these processes can be done by humans (and are in some places), it is likely that the fibers you purchase for yourself have been processed by machine.

**Retting:** Bast fibers, such as hemp or flax, are bound together in the stem of a plant with a gum-like substance. A process called retting removes the fibers. Much like the natural process of rotting, retting is a controlled way of using microorganisms and moisture to break down the cellular structure and remove the pectin surrounding the bast fibers, thus freeing them for textile use.

**Decortication:** Leaf fibers do not have the same level of gummy bond as bast fibers, so removal requires a different process called decortication. As the term is used in the medical world, decortication is the removal of a surface layer on an organ. Through crushing, beating, and scraping, the leaf is broken down, separating the fibers.

# Choose Your Fibers

Explore the characteristics of numerous natural and man-made fibers so you can be sure to choose the right one for your project.

| NATURAL FIBERS | | |
|---|---|---|
| **NAME** | **CHARACTERISTICS** | **NOTES ON PROCESSES AND USES** |
| Merino Wool | Strong, standard fairly soft wool; shrinks in wash | Standard wool; quite soft and inexpensive; spins well; accepts all dyes; good for knitting, crochet, weaving |
| Angora/Mohair | Soft; fuzzy, straight staple; shrinks in wash | Not as accepting of natural dyes; great for apparel as it is very soft; good for people who usually have allergies |
| Alpaca | Soft, decently strong depending on ply, shrinks in wash | Great for most things: dyeing, spinning, weaving, knitting, crochet; often used for apparel; hypoallergenic; very warm |
| Cashmere | Very soft; not as strong; shrinks in wash | Mostly used for apparel; accepts dyes well; very warm |
| Silk | Soft, shiny, strong but degrades with moisture and light; does not shrink too much in wash; absorbent, lightweight, and warm | Great for some apparel, mostly accessories, easily stained; accepts all dyes well; harder to print on; tough to spin |
| Cotton | Strong, standard natural fiber; ages well; shrinks in wash | Most popular natural fiber; used for everything; great for spinning, dyeing, printing, weaving, etc. |
| Linen | Gets softer with time; beautiful texture and sheen; can be brittle after washing; will mold easily; low elasticity; does not shrink too much in wash | Used for apparel and home goods; very light weight and cool; loses shape easily; tough to spin; easy to dye |
| Ramie | Strong, even when wet; resistant to bacteria and mildew; light fast; low elasticity | Does not dye well; very durable; great for fabrics that you do not want to mold (even outdoor); used for upholstery, filters, fishing nets; expensive to cultivate |
| Hemp | Soft; extremely durable even when wet | Highly sustainable plant; used for strength and durability; great for apparel and upholster; used in composite for automobiles |
| Jute | Tough; very durable; coarse | Used mainly for durability and strength: rope, rugs, twine, sacks |

| MAN-MADE FIBERS | | |
|---|---|---|
| **NAME** | **CHARACTERISTICS** | **NOTES ON PROCESSES AND USES** |
| Polyester | Strong; resistant to shrinking, mildew, wrinkles; holds pleats well; quick drying | Very popular synthetic fiber, mimics natural fiber well and is great for sewing and printing; cannot be naturally dyed or synthetically dyed |
| Nylon | Essentially plastic, toxic when broken down by fire; very strong; can mimic silk fairly well | Mostly used as rope, and is coarser if used for textiles; plasticy feel as in some bridal veils; used for industrial purposes and carpets as well; cannot be naturally dyed |
| Bamboo | Strong, absorbent, antimicrobial, very soft | Fibers cannot be spun, so is man-made; great for apparel and home goods; can be knit, woven, crocheted, dyed |
| Rayon/Viscose | Imitates silk most often, highly absorbent, cool, does not insulate, low elasticity | Apparel mostly for light weight purposes, linings, lingerie, hats, socks; other industrial and commercial uses; good for most textile processes, but NOT natural dyes |
| Acrylic | Feels like bulky wool, very good heat retention and fastness to light, very good shape retention, durability, easy care and quick dry | Acrylic yarns can be found very easily at the yarn store and are a good replacement for actual wool; can be quite soft and works very well for knit, crochet, weaving, synthetic dyeing |

## Man-Made Fibers

As you start stocking your yarn trees or studio shelves (slowly and as needed!), be sure to check out man-made and synthetic fibers—you don't need to stick to only natural fibers. They have many valuable and exceptional qualities because of their durability. Synthetic fibers are essentially plastic and so will last a long time and can be recycled. Because synthetic fibers and fabrics were originally made to mimic the feel of natural fibers, they often have beautiful drape and feel and can be a better option for outdoor or heavy-use projects.

For the past few decades, we have been conditioned to think that synthetic fibers are not as good as natural fibers, but as you purchase fabrics and fibers for your projects, don't discount man-made fibers; they add variety and value to textile design. After all, man-made fibers are continuously being developed and improved. Because of the production process (hot liquid polymers are extruded through tiny holes and then cool into solid fibers), man-made fibers have the added advantage of being as thick or as thin as desired. The first artificial fiber, Viscose was invented in 1894 as a substitute for natural silk. You probably remember those first fibers that didn't breath and pilled terribly; well, man-made fibers have come a long way since then.

Synthetic fibers account for about half of all fiber usage and have applications in every field of textile technology. From Saran used for shrink-wrapping, to spandex in sporting equipment, to Kevlar used in body armor, and carbon fiber used in the aerospace industry, synthetic fibers are indisputably vital. You probably won't need body armor in your studio, but you may be working on a project that does requires special yarn qualities. For example, if you are weaving an outdoor mat or hammock, you'll need materials that are resistant to damp and moisture and can withstand changing temperatures, bright sunlight, and other environmental stressors. Knowing the characteristics of synthetic fibers (see Choose Your Fibers, page 32) will add breadth and practicality to your projects.

**ABOVE** Shown here are examples of both natural and synthetic yarns on cones–can you tell the difference? Often, you can't!

## FYI | Natural versus Organic

When you hear the term "natural fiber," you tend to think that it must be good for the environment. However, cotton production has some negative environmental effects—it requires massive amounts of water for irrigation and up until recently, used harmful fertilizers and pesticides. More and more, we hear the term "organic" used to describe natural plant fibers, which means they are grown without fertilizers and pesticides, but we need to keep in mind how difficult it is for farmers to produce certified organic vegetation. While this does not mean you should not work with cotton, it does mean you should be open to exploring and researching exactly how natural fibers and synthetic fibers are created and the environmental ramifications.

These standard, natural fibers that are great to have around for experimentation and sampling.

## Stocking Your Home Studio with Natural Materials

While synthetic fiber production has changed greatly in the past decades to produce fibers that more closely mimic natural fibers, there is still a huge demand and desire for the "real thing." Natural fibers have a certain look and feel to them and are ideal for most textile media, including dyeing, felting, quilting, and almost every form of textile art described in this book.

To avoid over-shopping and filling your studio with too many things, we recommend shopping for each project as you start it. Your needs and desires for supplies and materials will change depending on your mood and the type of project you are creating.

However, it is helpful to have some of the very basic supplies on hand. Purchase the following items in neutral colors and use them for samples and experimenting.

- Unbleached muslin
- Cotton yarn in white and natural
- Wool yarn in white and natural
- Precarded roving in white and natural

You will use these items continuously, so it is worth it to have them on hand so that you can test dye colors, make sample garments and prototypes, and use them as "scrap" printing material.

We suggest spending some time at your local garment district or fabric store. Observe the drape, hand, thickness, and overall feel of different natural fibers from silks and fine woven cottons and linens, to jerseys and other knits. While we don't feel you need to stock your whole studio to start, when you see fabrics you love, whether very plain or highly textured or printed, buy a yard or take a sample. You can use them as inspiration for future projects. The same goes for yarns and fibers for felting and spinning; when something calls to you, it is wise to get a small amount. If you are starting a specific project, buy the amount needed.

## Synthetic Fibers Made from Natural Materials

Some synthetic fibers are made from natural plant materials, but processed through extrusion and often combined with chemicals. Bamboo and rayon are two fibers that fit this category.

Bamboo fibers and fabrics have become very popular; they are incredibly soft and strong and are considered sustainable, though it will depend who you ask. Bamboo grows fast and the fiber production does not emit the same amount of greenhouse gases as the production of synthetic fibers. Because bamboo is a natural fiber, it is often classified as a natural fabric, but remember the fiber must be processed to be usable. Bamboo fibers are only about 3 mm (⅛ inch) long and impossible to spin into yarn. Instead, the fibers are extracted from the pulp of the plant and often combined with chemicals to become useable.

Rayon is manufactured from regenerated cellulose, or plant material. Because it is produced from naturally occurring polymers, it's neither a truly synthetic fiber, nor a natural fiber; instead it is classified as a semi-synthetic or artificial fiber. In the textile world, rayon is also known as viscose. It is very versatile and can be blended well with other fibers to create fabrics that mimic the look and feel of natural fibers very closely. Because of this and the fact that is it is comfortable, soft, cool, and absorbent (although it does not insulate body heat), rayon is a popular fiber choice.

## POPULAR MAN-MADE FIBERS

**Nylon and Other Polyamides** The name nylon derives from New York and London because those are the cities where it was first used. It was created to resemble silk (which is lustrous and pleasant to the touch, but expensive to produce) and has been in use since 1938 for everything from toothbrush bristles to stockings. Nylon is a good choice for an outdoor project because of its resistance to the elements. Like all manufactured fibers, nylon is produced in a huge variety of gauges (diameter) and colors.

The other polyamide fiber-family worth noting is the aramids, which entered the United States market in the 1960s. Aramids are tough, strong and heat-resistant and therefore most commonly used in airspace and astronaut gear. A polyamide fiber, in a scientific structural sense, is a linkage of polymers, which are repeating structural cells.

**Polyester** Polyester earned a bad reputation when it saturated the fashion market in the 1970s. In truth, the qualities that made it ubiquitous in that decade make the fiber noteworthy and popular today. Fabric made of polyester is remarkably wrinkle-proof, and that can be of significant value. It is also produced in different weights and with various finishes and goes by the trade names Dacron and Kodel in the United States. In fact, polyester comprises 60 percent of all synthetics manufactured in the United States.

**Olefins** This class of polymer is made into both fiber and plastics. Two examples most readily used in textiles are polyethylene and polypropylene. These fibers are extremely hardwearing, which makes them useful for upholstery, rugs, and other high traffic fabric.

**Acrylics** Acrylics were first developed in the 1940s under the name Orlon. This synthetic fiber closely resembles wool in its visual and tactile qualities. Like wool, it is soft and has loft, but it is less expensive. Acrylic is often blended with wool and can be used to make anything from socks to carpets.

If you want to work with fake fur, then you will be using a modacrylic fiber, a relative of acrylic.

Here is an example of man-made fibers used for a beautiful woven blanket. The main fiber used here was bamboo. Using yarns of various weights created the honeycomb weaving structure; notice some of the very thin yarn is sparkly pink polyester.

## USING SYNTHETIC MATERIALS IN YOUR HOME STUDIO

Synthetics have come a long way since they were first produced. As we mentioned, the main goal of synthetic production is to imitate the look or feel of natural fibers, but at a much lower cost. Though natural fibers tend to be more popular, familiarize yourself with synthetic fibers so you can decide which you like best. Don't be afraid to mix natural and man-made fibers, and you'll have the best of both worlds. You may discover that certain fibers do just what you are imagining in your mind for a sculpture or a garment, but you'll need to try it out to see!

- At the root of it, synthetic fibers are plastic. This affects how the fibers react to certain things, such as heat. When exposed to high heat, they will melt.

- Synthetic fabrics are not easy to dye and will not accept natural dyes at all.

- Synthetics are great when you need strong, stretchy material such as spandex.

- Synthetics are long lasting and will not degrade like natural fibers.

- Synthetic fibers can be recycled into other things.

# Using Nontraditional Materials in the Home Studio

Traditionally, grasses and fibers have been used in conjunction with modern materials, such as plastic, to reflect the changing availability of materials in many parts of the world. For example, Senegalese Wolof women weave grasses and recycled prayer mats to create coiled storage baskets that combine traditional aesthetic with harder-wearing materials. There are many ways and reasons to try using nontraditional materials in your projects. Using nontraditional materials, such as plastic bags or wire, adds excitement to the most familiar of techniques and inspires new explorations.

**Fine Art**  Because fine art need not have any practical function, it is easy to incorporate nontraditional materials to add visual and tactile interest. There is no limit to what you can try, from using found objects to repurposed or recycled yarns, thread, and fabric.

**Weaving**  Weaving is an ideal technique for experimenting with different materials. The warp is the only fiber that needs to be strong and continuous; anything can be used as the weft. As long as the material fits in the shed, it can be woven into a strong warp. Try using fabric, plastic bags, strips of metal, rubber, or leather to make heavier rugs and mats. If you love the look of natural materials, try using un-spun materials such as reeds and grasses, straw, or even twigs. Some people even collect fur from their pets, spin it, and use it for weft in their weaving. It is usually best to use unstable or short pieces such as feathers as a supplemental weft to ensure the integrity of the piece.

**Knitting and Crochet**  Nontraditional materials are somewhat more difficult to use with knitting and crochet because of the need for material that is continuous and flexible enough to form small loops. A great material to try is light gauge wire or leather. This is especially beautiful for wearable art, like hair ornaments and jewelry.

**Embellishing**  Applique, beading, and other forms of embellishment are a great way to introduce fun and unusual materials to cloth. Because these techniques are used to decorate the fabric surface and do not effect the cloth's structural integrity, the range of materials you can use is virtually limitless, and you can find many things in everyday life such as buttons, beads, shells, coins, and feathers. Almost anything can be attached to the surface as long as it isn't so heavy that it will tear the fabric.

**Felting**  When felting fibers, it is possible to introduce non-wool materials in small quantities. The majority of the fiber has to be wool because the process of felting is dependent on the interlocking of microscopic cuticles found on wool. Synthetic yarns and foils can be introduced into the blend but are comprised of polymers that are smooth and cannot be felted to each other. If you would like to incorporate beads or sequins into your felted art, try stringing them on a piece of wool yarn that can be felted into the foundation.

This woven piece uses rope made for sailing! The finished fabric would be perfect for outdoors and has a chunky effect.

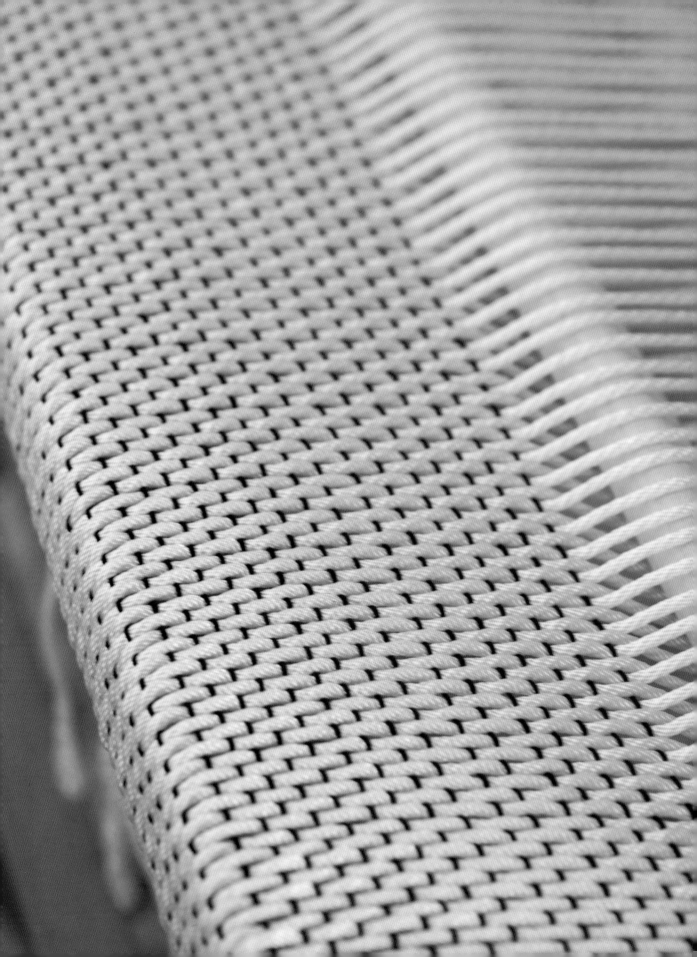

# Conduct a Burn Test for Fiber Identification

If you plan to paint or dye your woven cloth, you should know the fiber content of the cloth so that you can use the appropriate kind of dye. Likewise, if your goal is to felt or full your project, you will need to use materials that will respond to those treatments.

Some yarn will shrink a lot when washed, other yarns will not, so it is important to know what you are combining. If you are buying new yarn, your task is not too difficult because the fiber content is always indicated on the packaging. However, if you are using yarn you've had for a long time or were given as a gift, you will have a harder time. Because many synthetic yarns imitate natural fibers, it is sometimes hard to tell the fiber content of a yarn. To make it even more difficult, many yarns are a spun blend of different materials or have several different kinds of thread plied together. Sometimes this is done for added strength with a binding thread that keeps a loosely spun yarn from being too flimsy. In other cases, fibers are combined as a way to vary texture and finish.

While many experienced fiber-lovers can tell a protein fiber from a cellulose fiber, from a synthetic fiber, just by touching it, it's a good idea to conduct a burn test if you are not enthusiastic about surprises. As the name suggests, to do a burn test you must burn the fiber. Remember that some yarns will catch quickly so safety precautions are important.

- Avoid loose clothing, especially scarves and long sleeves.

- If your hair is long, put it up or tie it back.

- Use metal tongs or tweezers to hold the fiber instead of your fingers.

- Light the fibers over a sink or big bowl of water so that if they catch too quickly you can drop them in the water without hesitation.

Understanding how the three main categories of fibers, protein, cellulose, and synthetics, react to fire is key to helping you determine fiber content.

Yarns, threads, and fabrics made of different fibers behave differently under varying conditions, so it is important to know what to expect before selecting one for a project.

Though it is not the most accurate way of determining fiber content, burning is a simple and fun way to try to learn the identity of a mysterious fiber.

## Cellulose

*Cotton, linen, hemp*

A cellulose fiber will burn very smoothly and evenly, which is why candle wicking is made out of cotton (a cellulose fiber). The flame will be steady and yellow. The fiber will not self-extinguish, but if you let the fiber burn all the way (in a nonflammable container) the ash will be soft and light grey. The smoke will smell like burning paper.

## Protein

*Wool, silk, alpaca, angora*

When you light a protein fiber, it will burn briefly before self-extinguishing. The smoke smells like burning hair or feathers. The ash looks dark and irregular and turns into powder when crushed.

## Synthetics

*Polyester, rayon, acrylic*

There is greater diversity in the way synthetic fibers burn but there are some characteristics that remain constant. People usually notice the smell of plastic or chemicals when a synthetic fiber burns. The fiber self-extinguishes and melts into a hard black bead that can't be crushed. Because plastic can adhere to skin or fabric, be especially careful not to touch the remaining yarn until you are sure that it has cooled completely.

## STEP-BY-STEP BURN TEST

Consider creating a simple chart on foam core, cork board, or heavyweight material. Mark three columns with the following headings: protein, cellulose, and synthetic. Choose yarns, threads, and small fabric swatches that you know the fiber content of so you'll see how known fibers react and choose ones that you don't know the fiber content of so you can learn to identify the unknown.

1. Choose your threads, yarns, and fabric swatches. Cut two small pieces of each. Attach one of each into the left side of your chart. Save the other cuttings for the burn test. Refer to the safety precautions listed above.

2. Carefully hold a match to each of the corresponding cuttings one at a time. As you burn each one, take note of the characteristics. How quickly did it catch fire and burn? What smell was produced? What are the characteristics of the ash? Write your observations next to the cutting so you can deduct the fiber type. If you know the fiber type, write it next to the cutting.

3. As you fill in your chart, experiment with various yarns to become familiar with the defining characteristics of the various fibers and their reactions to fire. This chart can serve as a great tool in the studio, particularly if you add yarns from all your various projects and use it as a reference tool.

# Creating Textiles in a **Home Studio**

The next three chapters explore the fundamental ways to construct fabric: felting, knitting and crochet, and weaving. Through these foundations of textile arts, you can experience making something from nothing, from fiber to fabric.

The subsequent chapters explore design techniques such as screen printing, dyeing, sewing, embroidery, and appliqué. Let loose and experiment! Great textile art comes from combining processes.

CHAPTER

3

# Felting

**Felting is a simple technique of constructing fabric or three-dimensional objects through matting wool, fur, or other fibers together.** It is a wonderful way to make sheets of fabric, decorative accessories, fashion details, or even sculpture and ornaments. It doesn't require a lot of special equipment or space. Beyond the tools listed below, you'll only need soft and colorful roving, which is gorgeous to look at and a pleasure to work with! Roving is the name for the loose wool fibers as they come off the sheep.

There are two fundamental techniques; wet felting (page 47) and needle or dry felting (page 49). Felt doesn't have an internal structure the way that woven or knitted fabrics do. This makes it possible to construct felt into any form; it also lends it a special springiness. Felt is as warm as knitted wool, but has a special smooth appearance and is resilient to wrinkling and being crushed out of shape, making it an excellent fabric for hats. It also is sound and shock absorbent and can be made in about any color and thickness.

## Felting Tools

This is a wonderful textile handcraft for beginners, children, and experienced textile artists alike, and the initial outlay for tools and materials is minimal.

Wet Felting
- Roving or other wool fibers
- Oil-based soap
- Water
- Soft netting or mesh
- Rolling mat (bamboo) or felting stone
- Plastic tarp to protect work surface

Dry Felting
- Roving or other wool/synthetic fibers
- Felting needles, usually in a tool that can hold 1 to 12 needles
- Needle mat or foam pads

TIP | **Save Your Skin**

If agitating or rubbing the fibers together irritates or dries your skin, you can wear plastic gloves or you can felt without ever getting your hands wet! Place the roving (and plastic template if you are using one) inside a sealable plastic bag and apply the pressure and agitating strokes through the bag. When the felt feels tight, remove it from the bag, rinse it, and let it dry. No fuss, no mess!

This felt fabric was made through a method called wet felting. See the tutorial at the end of the chapter to learn how!

## Wet Felting

When viewed under a microscope, wool fibers have tiny directional scales or cuticles. Wet felting relies on the application of moisture, friction, and pressure to lock one fiber to its neighbor, bonding the surface. Although this sounds complicated, it is simply the rubbing of layers of roving with soapy water until they mat together (see tutorial on page 47).

If you are working in a very small studio space, you might want to work on a smaller scale and make felted items such as pin cushions, coin purses, key chains, and cell phone or camera cases. These smaller items are a great way to learn how to felt. In the wet felting tutorial, you'll learn to create flat felt fabric, which can be sewn just as if you are using it as fabric.

## Needle (Dry) Felting

Once you've mastered welt felting, you won't want to stop! When you are ready to work in more detail and add intricacy to your patterning, coloring, and forming, try needle felting.

Needle felting is based on the same principles as wet felting but offers greater detailing control. The felting needle is very sharp and barbed and is used to permanently tangle surface fibers into a base fabric. Use this technique to gradually build up a three dimensional object or to add details to sheets of felt or other fabric. Basically, you use the needle to add small amounts of roving as a way of "drawing" on the surface of a felted form or fabric. This is a wonderful way to create facial features on dolls, as well as a way to add color details and shading in two-dimensional art.

To create a three-dimensional figure, felt around an armature or other object or layers of roving to create the body and shape. Then apply roving to the outer surface to create details and make specific shapes.

## Nuno Felting

If you like how needle felting adds delicacy to felt, you may enjoy nuno felting! It is a special technique that uses a very fine or sheer backing fabric to stabilize and structure lightweight felt. The finished felt is sturdy enough to make into some clothing, but it is mostly used for making shawls and scarves. The beautiful thing about nuno felting is its softness without weight. This is achieved by felting on top of a woven fabric, typically silk gauze or other open weave fabric. You can use wet or dry or both techniques, and the finished felt lends itself to embellishments.

You will need a base cloth (usually silk gauze) and a rolling mat (or bubble wrap!) as a surface to help the fibers mesh. You can completely cover the base cloth or apply roving in a random or specific pattern. Consider felting on sheer fabric with patterning or a design already printed on it so you can use the pattern as a guide for where to add felted texture for visual and tactile interest. Follow the techniques for wet and dry felting on silk gauze or any fine fabric.

## Fulling

If you have ever accidentally washed a wool sweater in a washing machine, then you are familiar with fulling. Through the same process of applying moisture, pressure, and heat as in wet felting, the fibers matt together, condensing and causing the material to shrink. The difference between fulling and felting is that the fulling process is applied to fabric or ready-made garments rather than to loose fibers.

## TIPS Smoother Felting

- When making an armature for felting, use pipe cleaners instead of smooth wire. The texture of pipe cleaners creates a convenient gripping base for the roving to cling to and minimizes shifting around the frame.

- Because wool roving is expensive, sometimes you can use a combination of synthetic and natural fibers. If you decide to combine fibers, make sure at least half the fibers are natural or the material won't felt.

# Tutorial: Welt Felting in Your Studio

Wet felting is a very fun (and messy!) way to create fabric for constructing, embroidering, or even printing on. Through friction and heat, you bind loose fibers together. Depending on how many layers you use, you can make extremely durable and warm fabric.

## TOOLS

- Soft netting mat/mesh
- Bamboo rolling mat
- Tarp, tablecloth, plastic to protect your work surface

## MATERIALS

- Several ounces of roving in a variety of colors
- Boiling water
- Dish or olive oil soap (something soft on the hands)

## INSTRUCTIONS:

1. Cover your table or work surface to protect it from the water. Lay out your rolling mat on the table, giving yourself ample room.

2. With the roving in one hand, pull a small tuft away with the other hand until the fibers pull apart. Repeat to separate several fiber tufts and lay them out on your work surface. **[A]**

3. For the first layer, place several tufts side by side with the fibers all in one direction on the rolling mat. For the second layer, lay the tufts over the first, but in the opposite direction. This creates friction so the fibers felt together. **[B]**

4. Add three or four additional layers, alternating horizontally and then vertically. The more layers you have, the stronger the felt and the more felting time required. Five to six layers is good for a small sturdy piece of fabric. **[C]**

5. In a large bowl or sink, mix enough soap with the hottest water you hands can stand until the water feels slightly oily.

6. Cup the soapy water with your hands and wet the fibers. They need to be fully wet, but not resting in a puddle. **[D]**

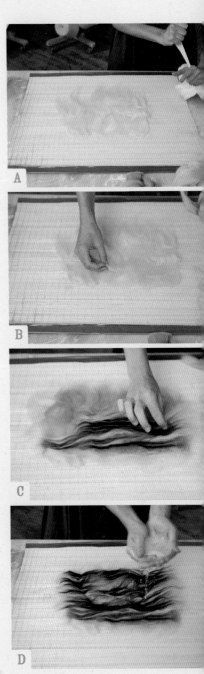

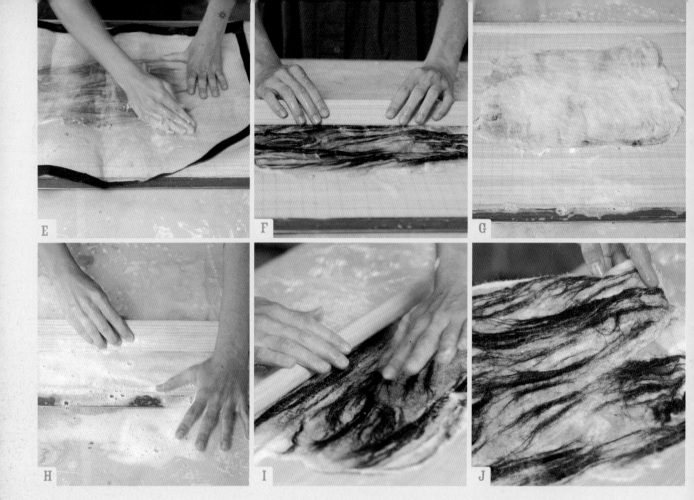

E    F    G

H    I    J

7. Secure the fibers by placing the netting mat or piece of mesh over them. Massage, knead, and rub the fibers with your hands over the mesh net in a circular motion until you see the fibers start to pill through the net. Once you see the pilling, you can remove the net; you will have applied enough friction to move onto the next step. **[E]**

8. Add more hot soapy water and continue to massage the fibers in circular motions. Continue adding hot water throughout the whole process as needed. Start to gently roll the felting mat with the secured fibers, allowing the thickness of the fibers determine the width of the roll.

9. Gently roll the mat so it agitates the fibers within. Careful not do be too rough, or it may make holes in your felt. **[F]**

10. Continue to gently roll the mat to agitate the fibers within. Periodically unroll the mat and flip the felted fibers so they are equally distributed. Pull the fibers gently to make sure the piece is strong; if the fibers start to pull apart, keep rolling. Once the fibers seem well integrated, you can press harder and flip the felt less; however, it is good to keep an eye on your work as much as you can to control the process. **[G, H, I]**

11. Once you like the look of the fibers and they appear well felted together, wash the piece in cold water. The temperature change will make the fibers grip each other! Rinse all the soap out and flatten it to let it dry. Now you have felted fabric that can be used as is or constructed into something else like a pillow or toy! **[J]**

# Tutorial: Dry Felting in Your Studio

Dry felting is a more detailed (and less messy) way to create fabric or objects. Through friction and the up and down motion of a needle moving through loose fibers, you bind them together.

Make a single ball of felt and use it as the starting point for all sorts of felted projects. Create one single beautiful bead or make several and construct a necklace. Experiment and sculpt your roving into shapes and sculptures.

## TOOLS

- Needle mat or foam pads
- Felting needles, usually in a tool that can hold 1 to 12 needles
- Plastic or tablecloth to protect work surface

## MATERIALS

- Roving or other wool fibers (You can add small amounts of synthetic fibers.)

## INSTRUCTIONS:

1. With the roving in one hand, pull a small tuft away with the other hand until the fibers pull apart. Pull apart several tufts in the desired colors.

2. Form a shape by wrapping the tufts around each other so the fibers crisscross. Or if you want to create a flat piece, lay multiple layers of tufts over each other as for wet felting. **[A]**

3. Position the fibers on the felting mat and carefully punch the felting needle(s) into the fibers. Punch the needle(s) at a 90-degree angle to the foam surface to help prevent them from catching on the fibers and breaking in your work. Remember that the needles are barbed and very sharp. **[B]**

4. As you felt the wool, constantly move the fibers around to cover all the areas equally. This is very important, as you must control the fibers!

5. Add more colors and layers of roving as your felt becomes more felted and restricted or until you achieve the desired size. Use the felted fiber as fabric or to create a three-dimensional piece, as for the bead **[C]**.

6. If you wish, add texture or patterns to the felted ball by felting smaller tufts onto the surface **[D]**.

7. Continuing adding to the aesthetic of the felt ball or bead until you are satisfied. You can use these as small toys for kids or even create a felt necklace by stringing together several felt beads using a very sharp needle and nylon thread **[E]**.

A

B

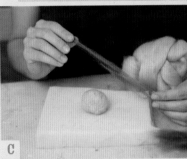

C

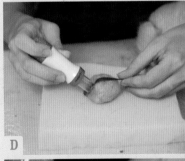

D

E

**CHAPTER 4**

# Spinning, Knitting, and Crochet

**The needle arts of knitting and crochet are a simple way of creating beautiful fabric.** The tools and materials are few and simple to store. They are portable and allow for experimentation through garment making and abstract sculpture. Knitting, by machine or by hand, and crochet are processes that create two-dimensional fabric from a one-dimensional continuous yarn. Consecutive loops (called stitches) are created and held "active" with needles or a hook by pulling the continuous yarn through the already-made, active loops. With each new loop or set of loops, the fabric is built.

Before knitting and crocheting, comes spinning, a very important step in the process of creating textiles. It is closely related to knitting and crochet. Spinning is the initial process in which fibers are spun into the yarns used for knitting and crochet. Of course, you can always purchase spun yarns in a tremendous variety of colors, weights, and textures

The world of spinning, knitting, and crochet is vast, with many techniques, styles, symbol systems, and histories. This chapter will give you a brief overview of these needle arts and the specific things you'll need for your studio if you wish to explore them further.

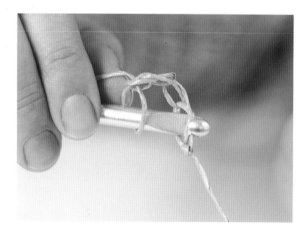

Crochet is a great skill that allows you to create fabric and garments, as well as sculptural and abstract pieces. The materials are few and require very little space in your studio. You can keep everything you need in a tote bag!

The women of the Patacancha community in Peru also spin their own fibers, mostly from alpaca using a drop spindle. *Photo: Kate Reeder*

## Tools and Materials

Spinning yarn and then using the yarns to create your own fabrics (from start to finish) through the processes of knitting and crochet is one of the most creatively rewarding textile experiences. It encompasses fabric design from the start with raw fibers to the finish, with the creation of fabric yardage through knitting or crochet.

For those who focus on textile art and design with ready-made fabric (screen-printed yardage or shibori dyed cloth, for example), you should consider adding spinning, knitting, and crocheting to your textile endeavors. These processes allow you to design from the absolute beginning and better understand the structure and therefore behavior of yarn and fabric.

Also consider combining techniques. Dye your own yarn or use strips of cut fabric to knit a chunky wall decor. Knitting and crochet can be used beyond traditional winter scarves and hats. Consider them as techniques that can be applied in many other ways.

We recommend keeping knitting, spinning, and crochet materials and equipment in your studio. The basics, listed here, are a minimal investment, easy to store, and versatile.

**Ball winder and swift** If you purchase yarn in skeins, you'll need to wind the skein into a ball, and these tools make it easy.

**Crochet hooks** With minimal expense, you can invest in crochet hooks in many sizes. They will come in handy for mending knit garments.

**Drop spindle** The drop spindle, either the top or bottom whorl, come in a variety of sizes and styles. Neither style is better, but you should try using different ones at the store to see which you prefer. Your first drop spindle should be heavy enough to keep a good spin going, but not so heavy that it's hard to operate. Discuss the options with the store clerk.

**Roving or Top** Make sure you have a variety of fibers in the form of roving or top in a variety of colors. Top is ready to be spun, with all the fibers aligned and carded. Roving needs to be carded before spinning; however, uncarded roving can be used to create a bulky knit or crocheted fabric or for both dry and wet felting. (see Spinning a Skein, page 58).

**Knitting needles** Stock your studio with straight and circular knitting needles in a variety of sizes. You might get a set of double-pointed needles for knitting in the round too.

**Yarns** Head to a yarn store and browse; you'll love it. What colors, textures, and fibers are you drawn to? Start collecting yarns slowly with a few basic skeins and don't overbuy as you will certainly fill your studio in time.

# Spinning Overview

Spinning is the creation of yarn from natural or man-made fibers. After harvesting fiber, it is the next step in textile creation. When you spin your own yarn, you have total control over the type of yarn you produce. You can select the type and blend of fibers, the colors, and whether or not your yarn has a mottled effect (see Space Dyeing Project) or uneven slub (see the yarn used for the Circle Scarf project). You have so much opportunity for creativity.

Spinning yarn is one of the oldest and most vital textile arts. Evidences of spinning in some form shows up in many historical artifacts, some from 20,000 years ago. The first methods of spinning involved taking animal fibers and rubbing them up and down the thigh. Over time, the need for yarn increased and the methods of spinning became more advanced to help meet the demand. Two tools, the spindle and distaff, were early spinning tools. The distaff was used to hold the unspun fiber, so hands were free to pull the fibers while spinning them. The spindle was a drop spindle, pretty much the same as we know it today. During the industrial revolution, the rate of spinning needed to increase, so while a drop spindle was quick, the spinning wheel, the tool that revolutionized spinning, was much quicker and efficient!

 **Art of Spinsters**

During the Middle Ages, many poor families in need of spun yarn kept the unmarried women and girls of the family spinning yarn in their free time, and they became known as "spinsters."

## SPINNING IN THE STUDIO

When most people think of spinning, they picture Rapunzel, who sat at a spinning wheel. A spinning wheel is a fairly large and expensive tool, certainly worth the investment if spinning becomes your passion. The Schacht Spindle Company sells small, portable, and quality spinning wheels at a good value.

If you aren't ready to invest in a spinning wheel, the drop spindle is also a popular way of spinning fiber into yarn, and it is small and inexpensive. We suggest starting with a drop spindle and exploring this first before moving on to a wheel. Learning to spin many kinds of fiber is fun and will keep you busy. Merino, alpaca, silk, and cotton all spin differently; and there is no replacing practice and trial and error for learning which fibers you like to work with most. See the tutorial on page 58 for a very brief introduction into the spinning world.

The following sections are about how yarn is used to create fabric by knitting and crochet. While it is true for all textile media, the world of knitting and crochet is especially huge. Our intention is to help you to understand the very basic principles of both knitting and crochet so that you can begin to use these media at home and further explore them for yourself. Your local yarn store will be a fantastic resource for learning more about yarns and for taking classes.

This skein was completely hand spun and wound using a drop spindle and merino roving top. Does it look that different from what you'd buy in a store? You can do it yourself!

## Understanding Ply

Yarn is spun by twisting fibers together in either a clockwise (S-twist) or counterclockwise (Z-twist) direction. The twists per inch (TPI) determine how tightly wound the yarn is. Single ply yarns are created with a Z-twist. To create thicker yarns, single ply yarns can be twisted, or plied together, using a "S-twist" to spin two already twisted yarns together. It is in the twisting together of different single-ply yarns that heavier, thicker, and multicolor yarns with blended fibers are produced.

## Knitting Overview

The history of knitting is fairly ambiguous. Since wool, silk, and cotton yarns degrade quickly, there are few knit items that date very far back. And, unlike weaving and spinning, which have very specific tools, knitting needles are simply pointed sticks. In addition, because yarn was a commodity, knit items were usually unraveled and re-knit when the garment no longer fit its owner until the yarn was no longer useable. No mention of knitting or crocheting appears in literary works until the fifteenth century, unlike weaving and spinning, which date back to humanity's oldest texts. Though the history of knitting is a mystery, there is no denying its cultural importance.

### HANDKNITTING

Flat knitting creates fabric with selvedges (edges). One set of two needles is used to construct row upon row of loops.

Circular knitting creates a tube, which can be used for the body of sweaters, socks, ornaments, and much more. Also known as "knitting in the round," you can

## Understanding Gauge

"Gauge" refers to the number of stitches in 4 inches (10.2 cm) of knitting. In hand knitting (and crochet), the gauge will vary depending on the yarn weight, needle size, and individual knitter. Always knit or crochet a swatch before starting any project and make sure it measures the indicated gauge measurements in the pattern.

To make and measure a gauge swatch:
1. Knit (crochet) a 4-inch (10.2 cm) square swatch.
2. Smooth out the swatch on a flat surface.
3. Use a tape measure to mark 4 inches (10.2 cm) across and 4 inches (10.2 cm) down. Count the number of stitches across and the number of rows down.
4. Compare your measurements to the suggested gauge measurements on the pattern.
   - If you have more stitches per inch, your stitches are too small. Try larger needles.
   - If you have fewer stitches per inch, your stitches are too big. Try smaller needles.
   - If you have more or fewer rows per inch than suggested, you might want to consider a different weight and/or texture of yarn. Or make length adjustments by knitting more or fewer rows as needed.

use one set of circular needles, which are connected by two ends by a flexible cord, or three or four double-pointed knitting needles, which hold active loops as you work your way around.

There are three very basic steps:

1. Cast stitches on.
2. Work the knit and purl stitches to create fabric.
3. Bind stitches off.

**Cast On** Every knit project is begun by "casting on," the creation of the first row of stitches. There are many ways to cast on. A knitter generally sets the width of the piece during casting on, but it can be made wider or narrower by increasing or decreasing stitches.

**Stitch Knitting** This involves two basic stitches, knit and purl, which create a wide array of patterns and styles. These two stitches are formed through the pulling of the continuous yarn through the front or back of an active loop. Though it seems simple, knitting can become quite intricate and detailed, as seen in the processes of intarsia, cable, or Fair Isle. These more intricate designs usually require a pattern, which break down the knit into "pixels." Patterns are also used in knitting to create shaped garments that require increasing, decreasing, and picking up stitches.

**Bind Off** The piece is completed by "casting off."

## Yarn Weight and Needle Size

Yarn is classified by weight, which refers to its thickness. There are bulky, worsted, sport, baby or sock, and fingering weights. The thicker the yarn, the fewer stitches it will take to knit 1 inch (2.5 cm); this is called gauge and is usually indicated on the packaging. If you have spun your own yarn, you will need to do a gauge swatch to determine how many stitches per inch it will knit.

You'll also want to try knitting projects with different size needles. Needles come in varying lengths. Straight needles are 10–14 inches (25.4–35.6 cm) long; and connected circular needles are much longer. Needles also come in sizes like 0, 1, 2, 3, etc. The larger the needle size, the thicker the needle. Thicker needles created larger size stitches.

Needles are available in many styles:
- Straight needles for knitting in rows
- Circular needles that are connected at one end for knitting in the round
- Double-pointed needles (or DPNs) for knitting in the round, especially at a small scale

## Machine Knitting

The knitting machine, along with advanced looms and spinning machines, played a very big part in the Industrial Revolution. William Lee invented the first knitting machine, the Stocking Frame, in 1589. His device was simple, and it replaced most production hand knitting. The opening of the first knitting factory quickly diminished the status of stockings as a luxury item. The machine eventually became the basis for all subsequent knitting machines capable of circular and ribbed knitting.

A knitting machine is built to hold hundreds of needles. A carriage, or cam box, travels left to right, creating new loops from the active loops, up to millions of loops per second. Knitting machines vary in complexity and ability, and therefore price and size. Some are manual, and others are electronic. You can create flat or tubular knits, as well as ribbing, and even whole garments on most knitting machines.

If you are considering purchasing a knitting machine for your studio, it is best to research your options. If possible, take a machine knitting class so you have a better idea of how the machines work and whether you enjoy the process. As a starting point, a 200-needle standard gauge machine allows for a lot of fun and exploration!

**ABOVE** This Brother KH860 is a standard gauge knitting machine. You can attach a second bed, or ribber, and hand-manipulate stitches.

**BELOW** Needles on a knitting machine move back and forth using your hand or the carriage, which moves left to right to create new loops.

---

### TIP | Warp and Weft

Did you know that knit fabrics have warp (lengthwise) and weft (crosswise) threads that run from finished edge to finished edge)? Weft-knits are most common; they have rows that run from left to right and each row of loops is dependent on the one before. Warp-knits are more complicated and are almost always created by machine. The yarns zigzag across the length of the created fabric, which means that when a hole is created the fabric will not "run" or unravel. Warp-knits are often used in delicate garments such as lingerie.

## Yarn Bombing and Other Contemporary Craft Uses

In the past decade there has been a huge increase in the use of fibers by contemporary artists. Yarn bombing is simply the use of knitted or crocheted pieces in street art or graffiti; it is often done during the night because it could be considered defacing public property. Once you start looking, you'll find textiles popping up in public art, which is often ephemeral. Though groups like Knitta and artists like Olek, who have been using "yarn bombing" in their work for some time, there has been a huge increase in this kind of "textile graffiti" around the globe. What would you tag with your knitting or crochet? Take a further look at the work of the group and artist mentioned above and you can learn a lot more about the potential political and conceptual meaning behind such activities.

## Crochet Overview

Crochet is more contemporary than knitting, dating back in literary texts to the mid-nineteenth century. The word crochet means "hook" in French, referring to the tool used to pull a new loop of yarn through a single active loop. Though knitting and crochet use the same basic principle, crochet only works one active loop at a time (with the exception of Tunisian knitting). Additionally, crochet stitches vary by wrapping the working yarn around the hook a variety of times before pulling it through the active loop. Crochet has a different set of symbols than knitting in terms of short hand and pattern reading. Gauge is as important in crochet as it is in knitting (see page 54).

Crochet is often used to create lace. It is a wonderful technique for finishing and embellishing, and it is also used to create jewelry and three-dimensional structures. Because of this, some people consider crochet to be a bit more free-form than hand-knitting. Generally, a machine cannot be used to create the look of crochet, and the inherent mathematical structure of crochet patterns has contributed to illustrating the theory of hyperbolic geometry!

# Tutorial: Spinning a Skein

Spinning with a drop spindle is a simple and convenient way to create your very own yarn, which you can then use to weave, knit, or crochet. You have the freedom to select the exact fiber content, weight, and look of the finished yarn. You can choose already dyed roving, dye it yourself, or spin natural yarn to be dyed after spinning. The possibilities are endless!

## TOOLS

- Drop spindle
- Carder
  (or use prepared fiber)
- Niddy noddy
- Two hands (yours!)

## MATERIALS

- 1 oz (28 g) Roving (either prepared or uncarded)

**ABOVE** Spinning a simple skein will require a drop spindle (a; **whorl spindle** is shown), roving (b), carders (c) (or already prepared roving), and a niddy noddy (d).

**TOP, RIGHT** Spinning yarn requires either a drop spindle or a spinning wheel. Shown here is a drop spindle with a bottom whorl, which is used in this tutorial.

## INSTRUCTIONS

### Carding *If you buy your roving, skip this section.

1. Begin with short lengths of roving. Spread them vertically across the width of one half of your carder.

2. Use the second half of the carder to brush (card) the fibers, pulling the carders in opposite directions from each another.

3. After several passes, your fibers should be evenly spread across the carder and appear much smoother than when you began. They should have been transferred to the working carder.

4. Grasp the fibers that hang from the end of the carder with both hands so that you can remove the roving as a whole piece.

5. Slowly roll back the fibers from the carder, being careful not to leave behind fibers or let them separate.

Carding aligns your fibers in the same direction so they are ready to be spun.

Your carded fiber should look like this.

Lift the aligned fibers at the edge of the carder to slowly roll off the roving.

You'll want all the fibers to come off the carder together. If fibers are getting stuck to the carder, you can use any long, thin tool to help you pull it off in one bunch.

This bundle of roving taken from the hand carder is called a *rolag*.

Here we will use a bottom whorl drop spindle. Shown is the carded rolag and starter yarn.

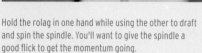
Hold the rolag in one hand while using the other to draft and spin the spindle. You'll want to give the spindle a good flick to get the momentum going.

Always maintain a V shape while drafting or pulling out the roving from the rolag to be spun. You do not need to pull very hard to draft, and you should be able to let the spindle do the work of the spinning.

Continue to draft and spin from the rolag until all of your roving is spun. You can then keep grabbing bits to spin more, change colors, or make only small bits at a time.

## Spinning

6. Hold the roving (from your carder, or pre-carded) in your dominant hand and grasp a small section with your other hand. Pull the section to thin it out without tearing it. This is called drafting. Depending on the weight or gauge of yarn you are trying to create, or draft, the thicker or thinner the rolls of roving will be.

7. Make a small loop at the end of the thinned strand and attach it to the hook on the spindle.

8. Drape the roving over the back of your dominant hand to keep it out of the way. Using the same hand, pinch the end of the section you've drafted for spinning. With the other hand, spin the spindle and watch the twist travel up the drafted section, turning it into yarn.

9. You'll know that you have twisted the fiber enough when you release the tension by bringing your hands closer and the drafted section kinks up on itself. This length of yarn is called the leader and is the beginning of the yarn.

10. Without unhooking the leader, guide it into one of the notches on the whorl and wind half the length onto the shaft of the spindle. Maintain some tension to prevent it from winding on with a kink throughout the spinning process.

11. Once you have wound the first half of your leader onto the shaft, bring up the second half through the notch in the whorl and under the hook. Repeat the process above.

## Finishing

After you've spun enough yarn, use your niddy noddy to create a small skein. A skein is a method of winding and organizing your yarn so it does not become tangled. In skein form, yarn can be easily washed or dyed, or you can wind a ball or bobbin from it.

Using a niddy noddy is a simple way to create a skein. It organizes the yarn and acts as a calculating tool for how much yarn is in the skein. Once you develop the V pattern, winding the skein goes quickly. Place your spindle with spun yarn in a container so it does not roll around.

**12.** Place your drop spindle with the spun yarn in a bucket or basket below you so that it does not roll out of control while you unroll the yarn.

**13.** Hold the niddy noddy securely in the middle and hold one end of the yarn under your thumb. Wrap the yarn as it unrolls from the spindle, to create two Vs. Continue wrapping in this manner, keeping the yarn tight to prevent if from slipping off the niddy noddy. **[A]**

**14.** Before taking the wound yarn off the niddy noddy, tie bits of yarn or ribbon around the bundle in several places as shown. **[B]**

**15.** After all the spun yarn is transferred from the spindle to the niddy noddy, it's time to take it off and wrap it into a skein. **[C]**

*(continued)*

A

B

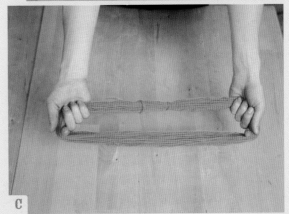

C

## Finishing *(continued)*

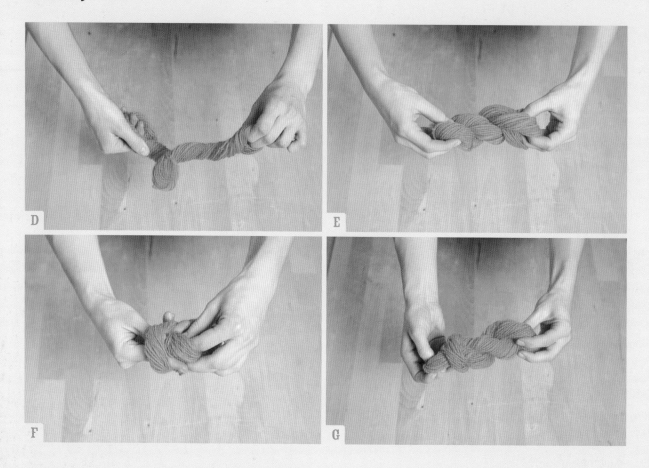

**16.** Twist the bunch of yarn, holding either side of the circle, until it starts to twist back onto itself. Bring your hands together, allowing the yarn to twist back onto itself, and pull one end through the other **[D, E, F, G].**

Congratulations! You have created you first hand-spun skein!

# PROJECT:

# Knitting a Circle Scarf

This scarf is a great first project; it's simple, straightforward, and teaches the basic principles of casting on, combining knit and purl stitches, and binding off. Keep in mind that varying yarn weight or needle size will produce very different looks (see page 55).

## TOOLS

- Circular needles (plastic or bamboo) in a size appropriate for your selected yarn (size 6 plastic needles, 18" [45.7 cm] long used to make project shown)
- Scissors
- Knit markers or short length of contrast yarn

## MATERIALS

- Yarn in weight and color of your choice, approximately 200 yards (183 M) (grey, slubbed alpaca wool used to make project shown)

## INSTRUCTIONS

This scarf is made using the stockinette stitch, which repeats the knit stitch throughout.

### Preparing and Knitting a Swatch Gauge

1. Decide the circumference that you want the scarf. Do you want it to just fit over the head and hug the neck tightly? Hang loosely? Wrap twice? Make note of the length and width measurements.

2. Knit a swatch to make a gauge test (see page 54). To check the gauge, cast on (see below) 10 stitches and knit 5 rows. Smooth the swatch and count how many stitches there are in an inch (2.5 cm).

3. What circumference measurement did you decide on? We've created a 40" (1 m) scarf, which wraps twice around the neck. Our knitting gauge was 3 stitches per inch (1 per cm). Multiply the desired circumference in inches by how many stitches you knit per inch to figure out how many stitches you need to cast on.

20" x 2 =40" (50.8 cm x 2 = 101.6 cm)

6" (15.2 cm)

## Casting On

4. To cast on, hold one end of the circular needle (or one of a pair of straight needles) in your left hand. Extend the cut end of the yarn three times the desired scarf circumference and mark the point for a slipknot. **[A]**

5. Make a slipknot at the measured marking and slide the knot onto the needle; tighten the knot close to the needle. Holding the needle up, you'll have two yarn ends (one long and loose and one connected to the ball of yarn). **[B]**

6. With your right hand, separate the two threads with your thumb and first finger so that the threads meet again underneath the tips of your remaining fingers. This should create a triangle. **[C]**

7. Holding the yarn taut, lower the tip of the needle to below your thumb to create a V. **[D]**

8. Move your needle under the thread wrapping your thumb and then over the opposite yarn wrapped on your first finger to pull a new loop through the thread wrapped on your thumb. Repeat this until you've cast on the correct number of stitches. Do not cast on too tightly, or it will make the first row difficult to stitch. **[E, F, G]**

9. When you've cast on the desired number of stitches, it's time to connect the ends to create the circle. (If you are knitting on straight needles, skip this step.) Flip the needles around so that you are now holding the side with the yarn ends in your right hand. (Of course, if you knit with the opposite hand, reverse these instructions.) **[H, I]**

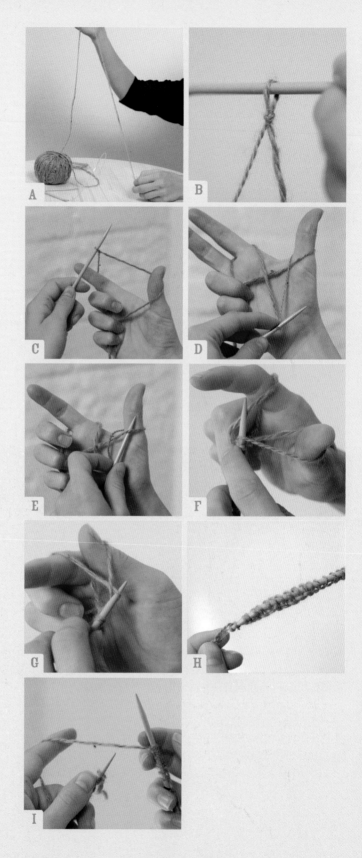

# Knitting

**10.** Make sure all your stitches are straight, not twisted, and facing the right way. Hold the yarn that is connected to the ball (you can trim the loose end) in your left hand, behind the needles. Close the circle by forming a knit stitch on the very first cast-on stitch, which should now be at the end of the needle in your left hand. Prepare to knit the first row with all knit stitches. Purl stitches, which are fundamental but are not worked in this project, are also explained.

**Knit stitch:** Pass the right needle through and behind the first stitch (or loop) so that the needles cross in the back. **[A]** Wrap the yarn counter-clockwise around the right needle. **[B]** Catch the yarn with the right needle **[C]** to pull the newly formed loop of yarn through the first stitch **[D]** and onto the right needle, forming the first stitch **[E]** and dropping the old stitch off the left needle. **[F]**Repeat until you have moved the stitches from the left hand needle to the right hand needle, forming a new row of stitches.

**Purl stitch:** Pass the right needle through, and in front of the first stitch (or loop) so the needles cross in the front. Wrap the yarn counterclock-wise around the right needle. Catch the yarn with the right needle to pull the newly formed loop of yarn through the first stitch and up and off the left needle onto the right needle, forming the first stitch and dropping the old stitch off the left needle. Repeat until you have moved the stitches from the left-hand needle to the right-hand needle, forming a new row of stitches.

**11.** Keep knitting until you get back to the beginning. Place a purchased knit marker or tie a different color yarn around the circular needle **[G]** to mark the location of the beginning of the row. (If you are using straight needles, simply flip the work and knit the next row.)

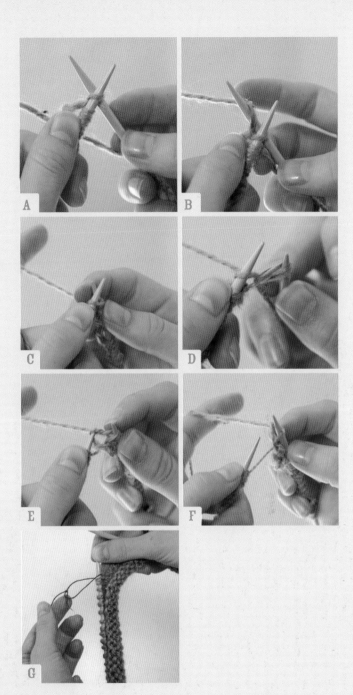

# Binding Off and Finishing

12. There are a few ways to bind off, but for this we suggest a double-wrap method that is used for finishing things that need to stretch. Knit a full row, but instead of wrapping the yarn to make a new loop once, you wrap it twice. **[A, B]**

13. Once you've double wrapped a full row, you can bind off. **[C]** Put your right needle through the first stitch **[D]** and transfer the stitch to the right needle, **[E]** unwrapping the double wrap. Do the same with the next stitch, **[F]** so that there are two very loose stitches **[G]** next to each other on the right needle.

14. With the left needle, go through the first stitch you moved to the right and pull it over the second stitch, dropping the first, leaving only the second stitch on the right needle.

15. Use the right needle to move the next stitch to the right side. **[H]** Again, use the left needle to pull the first stitch over the second and drop it. **[I]** Do this a few times, and you will start to see you are finishing the edge. **[J]** Continue to pull one stitch over the next until you get to the last stitch. For that last stitch, pull the thread through the loop and knot it close to the fabric so that it doesn't unravel. **[K]**

16. Wash the scarf with a little bit of soap and lukewarm water. To block (shape) it, lay it flat on a towel, pinning it in place so that it will dry to the shape you desire. Let it dry, and you're ready to go!

# PROJECT:
# Crocheted Ottoman

There are so many things that you can do with crochet! The patterns you can use are endless, and there are many ways to advance your craft. Here are basic instructions to make a great textured cushion. We love the neutral, chunky look. We used unspun roving for an over-sized crochet look, where stitches are visible. You'll need a ready-made cushion or a plain, beanbag-style ottoman. You can buy an inexpensive cushion and remove the current cover to refashion it or cover something you already own.

You can use knitting or crochet to cover almost anything and create a cozy decorative item. This seat in oversized roving is chic and comfortable for your living room or den.

## TOOLS

- Large crochet hook (we used size Q, 16 mm)
- Large or medium-size beanbag cushion
- Scissors

## MATERIALS

- 1 lb (455 g) of precarded Top (roving)

## INSTRUCTIONS

1. Form a slipknot near the end of the roving and place it on the hook. Tighten the knot up to the hook, but not too tight. Leave some tail to weave back into the piece when you are finished. **[A]**

2. Create a crochet chain using a chain stitch. Hold the hook in your right hand and the roving in your left. Pass the roving over the top of the crochet hook, above the slipknot. Wrap it over and into the notched hook to pull the roving through the slipknot to create a new loop. **[B, C]**

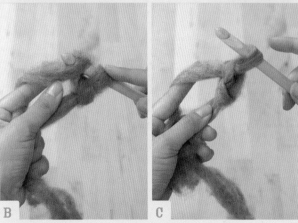

3. Repeat, wrapping the roving over and around the top of the crochet hook, and pull the new loop through the old loop. Do this ten times to create a chain ten stitches long (the bigger the initial chain, the easier to make the circle). **[D, E, F]**

4. Then connect the ends of the chain so you can begin working in the round, (called the ring). Form a slipstitch to connect the active stitch to the first stitch. Insert the crochet hook into the first stitch and wrap the roving over and around it. Pull this new loop through the first stitch and also through the old stitch on the crochet hook. This stitch is called a *slipstitch*, and used to connect chains and parts of the work without adding more stitches. **[G, H, I]**

5. Once the chain is connected, you can work in the round. The stitch you'll use for now is called *single stitch*. Like on the chain stitch, you'll start with the last loop made on the hook, insert through the top of the stitch in front of the loop, wrap the roving over the hook, and pull the roving through the stitch. You'll now have two loops on your hook. Wrap the roving over the hook again and pull it through the two loops on the needle at once. You now only have one loop on the hook, and you completed your first stitch. **[J, K, L, M]** Placing a stitch marker on the single stitch will help you know where the round starts and ends.

6. Move to the next chain stitch (the one on the left of the hook). Repeat the single stitch 9 times. You should now be at the beginning of your round, by the stitch marker, and you should have worked 10 stitches. The last stitch of every one round is the stitch just before the stitched marked. To start a new round, your first single stitch we'll be on top of the stitch marked. **[N, O]** Don't forget to replace the stitch marker after you start a new round.

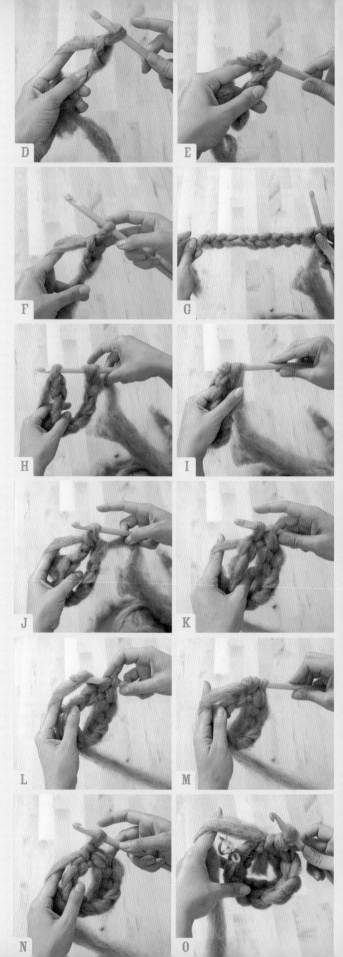

7. For the rest of the project, you'll use the single stitch. The idea here is to increase and decrease the number of per round stitches to mold the fabric to the shape of the round ottoman.

If in the first round you have 10 stitches, you'll want to increase 10 stitches per round while making the circle: work 2 single stitches onto the same stitch of the previous round.

**Example:**
*Round 1:* Make 10 single stitches into the ring (10 stitches).
*Round 2:* Make 2 single stitches into every single stich from previous round (20 stitches).
*Round 3:* Make to 2 single stitches into first single stich from previous round and make 1 single stitch into next; repeat 10 times (30 stitches).
*Round 4:* Make 2 single stitches into first single stitch from previous round and make 1 single stitch into next 2; repeat 10 times (40 stitches).

8. Work in round, increasing stitches until you're happy with the dimensions of the circle formed. Now start building the body of the ottoman. You'll work in round using the single stitch, without increasing stitches. Work as many rounds as needed to created the body of the ottoman. **[P, Q, R, S]**

9. When you're happy with the height of the otto-man, you're ready to start working on the circle of the base. You'll have to decrease the number of stitches per round to build the bottom circle. To decrease, you'll work two stitches together, at once. Insert the hook into the next stitch and pull through (you now have 2 loops on the hook). Don't work them and insert the hook into the next stitch and pull through again (you now have 3 loops on the hook). Wrap the roving over and around the hook and pull through the 3 loops at once. To decrease in proportion, you'll follow the same pattern that you've used to increase. **[T, U]**

**Example:**
*Rounds 5–10:* Work single stitches around (40 stitches).
*Round 11:* Work 2 stitches together, single stitch in next 2 stitches; repeat 10 times (30 stitches).
*Round 12:* Work 2 stitches together, single stitch in next stitch; repeat 10 times (20 stitches).
*Round 13 :* Work 2 stitches together; repeat 10 times (10 stitches).

10. When you finish the base circle, you should finish with a round with the same number of stitches as the round you started. To finish, make a slip stitch into the beginning stitch of the previous round, cut the roving (leaving a tail), and pull the roving through the last loop. **[V]**

# CHAPTER 5

# Weaving

**In contrast to processes such as knitting and crochet that use one continuous thread, weaving uses two sets of thread interlaced at perpendicular angles to create a grid.** Woven fabrics are classified by the manner in which warp (the vertical threads that are woven into) and weft (the horizontal threads being woven) threads cross each other. There are three fundamental weaves with many variations of each; they are the plain, twill, and satin weaves. They all involve the same basic steps:

1. Raising alternating warp threads to create an opening called the shed, through which the weft threads can pass

2. Using a shuttle (page 76) to pass the weft into and through the shed

3. Lowering the shed

4. Battening the weft, row by row, to form fabric

In this chapter, we've compiled lists of the important vocabulary terms and tools, we've described and illustrated the parts of a loom, and we'll take you through each step of the weaving process. Though setup can be laborious, the process of weaving is extremely meditative and satisfying … but it's not for the faint of heart!

# A Brief History of Weaving

As people started farming and domesticating animals during the Neolithic period, plant and animal fiber became available for spinning yarn. Weaving tools such as the vertical weighted loom were developed from the practice of hanging warp threads from a tree and holding them taut to the ground with stones. The Back Strap Loom, which is still widely used across South and Central America, allows the weaver to travel with the loom. The warp threads are tied at one end to a stationary object and the other end to the weaver's body in order to create and control tension.

**ABOVE** In South America, back strap weaving is still used widely. Shown here is a woman in a community in Patacancha, Peru. She works as part of a new collective with the Awamaki Organization.
*Photo: Kate Reeder*

**RIGHT** On an 8-harness floor loom such as the Harrisville shown here, you can create simple or highly complex woven fabrics.

By the twelfth century, the first foot loom, the forerunner of the modern power loom, was invented in Persia; it was the first loom to adopt the modern horizontal form. It mechanized the raising of the warp threads, which quickened the process by freeing the hands to throw and catch the shuttle. In the middle ages, the loom became a ubiquitous presence in homes in the western world. The word *heirloom*, which refers to a valuable object that has belonged to a family for several generations, derives from the words "heir" and "loom" and reflects the importance and value of weaving.

Looms went largely unchanged until the eighteenth century, when weaving and spinning inventions helped spark the Industrial Revolution and marked the transition from domestic craftsmanship to organized industry. Today, computer-controlled and powered Jacquard looms govern each thread in the warp individually, producing fabrics with complicated and organic designs.

# Glossary of Weaving Terms

Understanding the terminology associated with weaving helps simplify the process.

## WEAVING TOOLS

Weaving does require tools and ample space in your studio; however, you don't need to rush out and buy everything on this list. In fact, it's a good idea to take a class or spend time testing different style looms before you purchase anything. You'll most certainly want some type of storage because the beauty and diversity of the yarns will compel and hook you, once you start weaving, to stock your studio.

**The Loom** A loom is your most important investment. Regardless of how serious and in-depth you want to get with weaving, there are many options. Take time to learn and experiment with different types. You'll want one that allows for some growth in the craft. Following is a basic definition of the parts of the loom and a list of looms, from smallest in size and least expensive to largest in size and most expensive.

**Parts of a Floor Loom**
1. Castle
2. Cloth/Front beam
3. Warp/back beam
4. Warp
5. Brake
6. Beater
7. Reed
8. Harness/shaft
9. Heddles
10. Treadles
11. Tie-up
12. Bench
13. Cloth

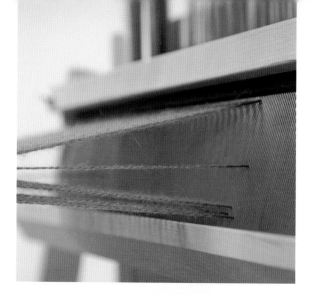

**Back beam** The back beam provides structure for the warp to travel on a horizontal plane through the heddles. It also serves to tension the warp when the loom is dressed and the warp is tied on to the cloth beam.

**Castle** This is the topmost part of the loom.

**Cloth beam** This is the front beam that sits below your woven cloth, to which the front warp strings are attached with an apron stick. As fabric is made and the warp is advanced, it is held on the cloth beam.

**Front beam** The warp travels over the front beam to the cloth beam. The front beam helps maintain a horizontal plane for the warp.

**Warp beam** The warp is attached to the warp beam.

**Apron stick** This is the rod to which the warp threads are tied to in order to be wound onto the beam.

**Beater** A vertical structure that holds the reed. The beater travels in an arc and lends weight to the weaver's battening or packing the weft.

**Harness or Shaft** This is the frame(s) that holds the heddles. It is raised and lowered to move the warp threads up and down.

**Heddles** These are the looped wires or cords with eyes or openings in the center through which the warp yarns pass. The heddles are suspended from the harness or shaft, and there is one heddle for each warp.

**Reed** This is a comb-like piece that spaces the warp threads and pushes the weft into the cloth, which sits within the beater.

**Treadles** These are foot pedals that are attached to the harnesses to move the warp up and down, opening the shed and making it possible to execute the desired woven pattern.

**TOP** By raising heddles with the treadles at your feet, you create the "shed" or opening through which a shuttle will pass from one side to the other.

**MIDDLE** The shuttle passes the weft thread through the shed, creating fabric.

**BOTTOM** The beater moves back and forth, packing weft threads into place. How hard the weft is beaten helps determine the fabric density.

**Rigid Heddle Loom** Rigid heddle looms are usually small and easy to store, so if space is limited and expansive weaving width is not imperative, this loom is a good option. This type of loom has a heddle system that conveniently also serves as the beater, but it only works two sheds. This feature makes the loom a simple one to master, but it also reduces the range of patterning. With a little creativity, you can still make beautiful and varied designs by experimenting with different threading sequences. For example, by skipping or multiplying ends in a dent, you can control the density across the cloth to create a varied texture in the surface. Alternately, dressing the loom with a multicolored warp can create intricate plaids that simulate weave structures only possible on more complex looms.

**Table Loom** Unlike rigid heddle looms, table looms have a free-hanging heddle system with four to sixteen harnesses. Generally they are small, compact, and easy to store and are only slightly simpler than a floor loom. Most notably, treadling on a table loom is done by hand levers instead of foot pedals, which makes it necessary to use the loom on a table or stand, and gives it its name. Manipulating hand levers does slow down the weaving process because the weaver must alternate between the tasks of passing the shuttle and opening the next shed; however, beginning weavers might find it helpful to see the levers in front of them instead of blindly pressing pedals with their feet. Another advantage for beginning weavers is that the harnesses stay up until the next shed is opened, so keeping track of the pattern is easier.

**Standard Multi-Harness Floor Loom** Standard floor looms are popular models. They come in sizes from large and heavy to quite small, and many fold. A folding floor loom is a great option if you are looking for speed but are tight on space. Once folded, they take up far less room in the studio. They have between four and sixteen harnesses and use a foot treadling system for raising a shed. If you are purchasing a folding floor loom for the sake of saving space, there are other ways to weave wider cloth with smaller floor looms.

Floor looms are sturdy, long-lasting machines. They have detachable chains or cords connecting treadles to harnesses, a system that allows custom tie-ups and makes it possible to raise multiple harnesses by depressing a single treadle. There are two types of standard floor looms, a jack-type loom that creates a rising shed and a countermarch or counterbalance loom that creates a sinking shed. The end results are pretty much the same whether the shed rises or sinks, except that advanced techniques such as weaving double cloth are more difficult on a sinking shed. Most American looms are jack-type, so they are readily available to the American weaver.

**RIGHT** There are many table loom options out there. This is made by Schacht Spindle Co.

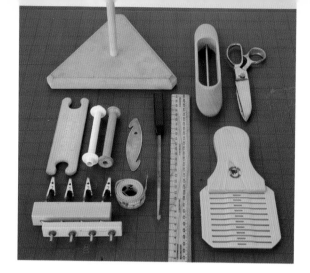

**Dobby Loom**  Dobby looms are generally quite expensive and computerized. They are suitable for advanced weavers who are looking to explore and create complex designs with increased speed. Before the invention of the dobby loom, the system for raising a shed relied on two people working in unison, one to raise the shed and the other to pass the shuttle. The person responsible for manually raising the harnesses for the shed was called a "draw boy," and the word "dobby" is derived from that term.

The dobby is an actual device (in place of treadles or levers) that raises the harnesses. Because the number of sheds grows exponentially with the number of harnesses, the dobby is extremely useful; it eliminates the use of treadles that limit the number of possible tie-ups, making all sheds available all the time. Speaking practically, what this means is that the pattern repeat need not be memorized or referred to continuously because the loom is preprogrammed to execute the pattern. The loom may be operated through man-power or through a dobby pedal that raises the numerous harnesses effortlessly.

**Shuttles & Bobbins**  A shuttle is key to the weaving process. It holds the weft yarns as it is passed back and forth through the shed, between the warp.

- The **flat** or **stick shuttle** is a flat piece of wood with notches on the ends to hold the weft yarn. Cheap to buy and easy to make, weft is wound around the stick and manually unwound at each pick.

- A **rag shuttle** resembles two flat shuttles connected by short wooden pegs. It can hold quite a lot of thick yarn or fabric weft.

- A **ski shuttle** is similar to a rag shuttle but has a ski-shaped bottom that makes it easier to slide through the shed.

**Miscellaneous Tools**  Some tools you'll need to get started; others you'll need if you weave regularly.

- A **ball-winder** winds balls of yarn in a neat way.

- A **bobbin winder** is necessary to wind yarn onto a bobbin. It can be electric or manual.

- A **lease stick** is used to keep the cross defined during the loom-dressing process, especially the beaming of the warp and the threading of heddles.

- A **pick-up stick** is used in techniques when individual warp ends are raised to the surface manually.

- A **raddle** is used to dress the loom back to front and for spacing the warp while winding it onto the warp beam.

- A **reed** comes with a loom, but you'll want a variety in different densities to accommodate finer or thicker warp yarns.

- A short and wide hook, called a **sley hook** or a **fish**, is used for threading or sleying the reed.

- A **temple,** also called a **stretcher**, is an extendable wooden or plastic stick with teeth at the ends. It is used to keep the width of the fabric constant.

- A **threading hook** is helpful for threading heddles.

- An **umbrella swift** expands to fit any size yarn skein so the skein can be wound into a ball. An alternative is having a friend hold a skin in their outstretched arms as you wind the warp, but this tends to strain a friendship unnecessarily.

## Yarn

The beauty of weaving is due in part to the wonderful variety of yarns and other materials suitable for it (see chapter 2). You'll find that stocking up on yarn is much too easy! Yarn is packaged or sold in skeins, balls, cones, and tubes. None are better than the others; your preference might just depend on storage.

**Skeins** A skein of yarn is a loose loop that is tied in several places. It is the only format from which it is not possible to wind bobbins directly. A skein must be wound into a ball or used from an umbrella swift.

**Balls** Smaller quantities of yarn, readily found in yarn stores, are often wound into balls. It is best to use a ball of yarn starting with the end at the center. That way the ball will not roll around on the floor as you wind a warp or bobbin, collecting dust and getting tangled in chair legs.

**Cones** A cone often contain thousands of yards of yarn wound around a cone-shaped core.

**Tubes** A tube is the same as a cone but slightly less stable for winding bobbins or a warp. It may require a cone stand to stabilize it during use.

## Weaving Vocabulary

An understanding of the following terms is necessary to understanding the weaving process.

**Balanced Weave** - A basic style of weaving in which the same number of threads per inch are used in both warp and weft

**Cross** A method of winding warp into a figure "eight"

**D.P.I. (dents per inch)** The number of slots in one inch in a reed

**Draft** The instructions for dressing the loom and weaving a particular pattern

**Draw-in** The pulling in of selvedges during weaving

**E.P.I. (ends per inch)** The number of ends per inch in the warp

**Fiber** The raw material used to make yarn

**Finishing** Techniques used to treat fabric after it has been woven, including washing, brushing, hemming, knotting, etc

**Fringe** The unwoven warp on the beginning and/or end of the woven cloth; also called tassels

**Pick** A shot, or passage of a shuttle through the shed

**Selvedge** The finished edges of the woven cloth

**Set** The number of ends in one inch of the fabric you are weaving

**Shed** This is the tunnel-like opening between the raised and lowered warp threads. The shuttle, with the weft wound on it, is passed through the shed to create woven fabric

**Shot** Passage of a shuttle through the shed

**Sley** The threading of the reed

**Take-up** The distortion on the sides of woven cloth caused by the process of weft curving over and under the tensioned warp ends

**Warp** The yarns that are being woven into, which run vertically on the loom

**Warp end** A single tread in the warp

**Weft** The yarn carried by the shuttle, which is woven into the warp and runs horizontally

# Choosing Yarn

Selecting yarns for weaving is not only a matter of aesthetics, but also of practicality. Floor mats, furniture upholstery, and other outdoor wovens need to be made from materials that can withstand prolonged exposure to the elements without deteriorating. A baby blanket, on the other hand, should be both very soft and supremely washable. In most cases, the final usage determines the kind of yarn you choose, and there are a couple of considerations that should be factored into any decision.

## WARP

Some yarns, regardless of the project, are not a good choice for a warp. They may have one or more properties that make it difficult to get the desired tension or a good shed. Before deciding on any warp yarn, test it by duplicating conditions that resemble the warp on the loom.

- Test for strength by breaking the thread. The thread will break in most cases because after all, it's just thread. So how can you tell if you are strong or the thread is weak? The best way to judge is by listening to the sound the thread makes as it breaks. A higher-pitched "ping" indicates a higher tension upon breaking and a stronger thread. A lower-pitched "phut" indicates a lower tension and a weaker, or under-spun, yarn.

- Another consideration is the stretchiness of the yarn. Because the yarn is pulled in order to tension it on the loom, you may run into problems, or surprises, with a stretchy yarn. It can be hard to tell just how much to pull the yarn when tying the warp onto the loom if it has a lot of give. Even if you do manage to equal the tension all the way across the warp, it might still be difficult to tell just how much to tension the warp every time you advance it, which could lead to inconsistency. Finally, a stretchy warp will look quite different once it is removed from the loom.

- The texture of the yarn is also important. There are various yarn finishes that make a yarn nubby, fuzzy, loopy, slubby, or otherwise textural, which can be quite a treat when used as the weft, but a problem when used as a warp. Textured yarns are also difficult to get through a reed's dents, and the thicker yarn sections can mat together on the loom through the agitation of continuous beating. The matting can then obstruct the shuttle's passage through the shed. If you do use textured yarn, space the warp ends accordingly to minimize friction.

## WEFT

You do not have to follow as many rules when it comes to choosing weft yarn. Although the strength, elasticity, and texture of the yarn will still affect the look of your cloth, the weft yarns are not subjected to the same tension, nor do they go through a reed or heddles. The weft affects the finished fabric, but not the actual process of weaving or the set up of the loom.

You can essentially choose anything that is long enough for a weft, including plastic bags, paper towels, paper, wire, or rope, for example.

When it comes to choosing yarns, however, consider the relationship of the weft to the warp. If you are trying to make a usable or wearable fabric, it is best to choose similar yarns so the shrinkage is the same and you have a balanced weave. If you were to choose cotton for the warp and wool for the weft, one would shrink more than the other. Similar yarn weights are helpful too. Ultimately, it is the relationship between the warp and weft that is most important.

Shown here is the Cricket Loom, made by Schacht Spindle Co.

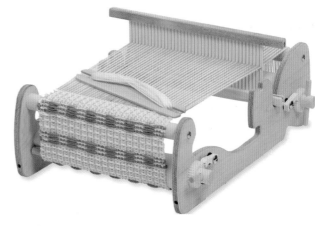

# Tutorial: The Weaving Process from Start to Finish

Weaving itself is quite simple, mostly because all the work is done before you ever start weaving. You need to plan the project and then set up the loom. Planning the project involves some math, and setting up the loom requires patience and attention to detail. You might want to start with a weaving draft (page 96), which indicates all the set up requirements to weave a particular pattern. The basic steps are listed here, then explained in detail in the following pages, and are finally demonstrated through a step-by-step weaving project:

1. Use weaving formulas to determine how much warp and weft yarn you need.
2. Wind the warp.
3. Dress the loom, which includes beaming the warp, threading the heddles, sleying the reed, tying on, and tying up.
4. Wind a bobbin, prepare the shuttles, and finally, weave.

## WEAVING FORMULAS

Weaving leaves little to guesswork, thanks to several foolproof formulas. We use the ones from Deborah Chandler's excellent book, *Learning to Weave*. They help you determine how much yarn to buy for both warp and weft, and how long, wide, and dense a warp to wind.

The first step in any weaving project is to determine your warp needs, how long each yarn should be and how many across you'll need to create the desired width, before winding the warp and dressing the loom. Remember, warp yarns are the vertical ones, tied taut on the loom and then lowered or raised to create patterns. Use the formulas below to ensure that you have enough yarn to make your finished project the size and shape you want.

**E.P.I or Warp Density Formula** This formula helps you determine sett, or ends-per-inch requirements. The ends are the warp or horizontal threads in the woven cloth. Sett directly relates to the gauge or weight of the selected yarn. You'll need more fine yarn than thick, nubby yarn to weave the same dimension fabric.

**E.P.I. (ends per inch) for the chosen yarn:** Wind the yarn around 1 inch (2.5 cm) of a ruler at the desired density of the finished cloth. Count how many times you wound the yarn around the ruler within the 1 inch (2.5 cm). This number is the sett or E.P.I.

**P.P.I (picks per inch [cm]) for the chosen yarn**
The P.P.I (picks per inch) is essentially the same as ends per inch, or the sett, but it pertains to the weft instead of the warp. Picks per inch indicates the number of weft shots of the chosen weft yarn in 1 inch (2.5 cm) of woven fabric. There are variables that affect this, so there is not a clear formula, but you can weave a bit of fabric and count the number of picks (passes) that creates 1 inch (2.5 cm) of woven fabric. This is similar to the idea of knitting a gauge swatch.

**D.P.I. Formula** You'll need to know D.P.I. (dents per inch) to determine the sley order. Simply count the number of slots in 1 inch (2.5 cm) of the reed you will be using for the project. A 12 dent reed, for example, will have 12 dents (or slots for the warp) per inch across the reed.

**Sley Order Formula** To determine sley order, divide E.P.I. by D.P.I. You may want to round your E.P.I. up or down depending on the D.P.I. of your reed. For instance, if your reed has 12 slots (or dents) per inch, you may want to wind a warp that will divide into it easily; if your ruler test leaves you with an E.P.I. of 25, round it down to 24. This way when you divide E.P.I by D.P.I, you will get 2 ends-per-dent. Keep in mind that your sley order (or how many ends you put through each dent in the reed) helps determine the density of the cloth. Two or more ends in each dent make the threads closer together (denser), while one end per dent leaves them further apart.

This means you will thread two ends of the warp through one dent in the reed. If you did not round the E.P.I. down, you would have to thread 2 ends-per-dent over 11 dents, then thread 3 ends in the twelfth dent of every inch. This is not difficult but it does require concentration.

**Warp & Weft Needs Formulas** Before you can do anything, you need to know how much yarn to buy to complete the project. The number of warp threads that are side by side on the loom determines the finished width of the project. You'll need to decide on the desired finished length and finished width and then calculate how much yarn or thread you'll need. You'll also need to add the following:

*Take-up* Your weaving length will decrease by about 10 percent of the desired finished length including fringe length.

*Shrinkage* depends on fiber, so wash a sample first. Usually it is approximately 10 percent of the desired finished length including fringe length, so round up to the nearest inch. Wools and cottons will have the most shrinkage from washing, while synthetics will have hardly any.

*Loom waste* is about one yard (0.9 m).

*Draw-in* is 10 percent of your desired weaving width. This idea is similar to take up, but along the weft instead.

*Total warp width on the loom* = Desired width + draw-in + shrinkage

*Total warp length on the loom* = Desired width + take up + loom waste

***Formulas for Warp Needs:***

*Total length of warp* = Desired length of finished project + fringe length + take-up + shrinkage + loom waste

*Total warp width on the loom* = Desired width + draw-in + shrinkage

*Total ends needed* = Warp width on loom + E.P.I.

*Total warp needs* = Total ends needed + Total length of warp

*Total warp width on the loom/Length of one shot (or pick)* = Desired width + draw-in + shrinkage

*Shots needed to weave 1 inch (2.5 cm) of fabric* = Length of one shot (above) x shots per inch (2.5 cm) of fabric × the desired finished length of the project

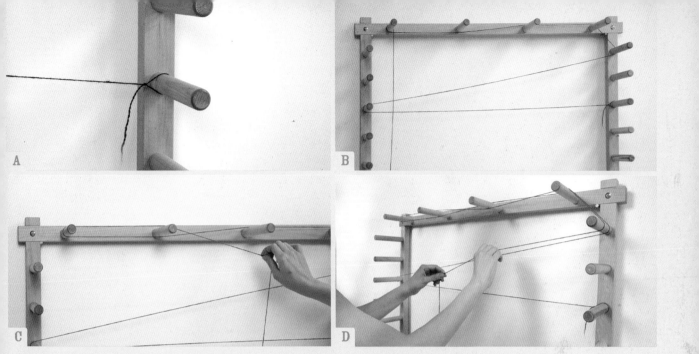

## WINDING THE WARP

Once you have used the formulas to determine how much yarn you need, it's time to wind your spun (page 58) warp yarn. (The warp is the yarn you tie onto the loom before you start to weave.)

After determining the E.P.I (ends per inch) for your warp yarn and the desired width of your project, you will use a warping board to measure out your warp. (For calculating E.P.I., see page 79.)

A warping board or warping mill helps you count out the number of ends needed to create the desired width. You'll also use the warping board to measure out the warp by creating a "cross" or "figure eight" across the top to keep the warp lengths organized. Use a warping board for projects that are up to 13 yards (11.9 m) long; longer projects are best wound on a warping mill.

Most warping boards are 1 yard (0.9 m)-wide between the pegs on the left side and the pegs on the right side. This makes it easy to keep count, because you'll zigzag from left to right as needed to obtain the correct length warp. For example, if your project requires a 5-yard (4.6 m) warp, you'll want to trail the yarn between the pegs five times.

### How to Wind the Warp

1. Place your yarn ball in a basket or cone between your feet as you stand facing the warping board, which should be hanging on a wall.

2. You'll want to work your yarn across the top of the board. If your warp is five yards (4.6 m) long, you'll make five passes between the pegs. Tie your thread end with a double knot to the correct peg. **[A]**

3. Using your dominant hand, trail the yarn across the warping board and around the opposite left peg. Travel back to the right side and around the peg above the first peg. Continue as many times as you require yards of warp for your project. **[B]**

4. When you round the last peg on the vertical part of the frame, continue horizontally crossing the yarn over the first peg and under the second peg.

5. Continue trailing the yarn across the top and under and around the last peg on the horizontal part of the frame, wrapping it back across the top, over the next peg, and under the following peg. This is called the cross, and it is important because it keeps your warp in the intended sequence. **[C, D]**

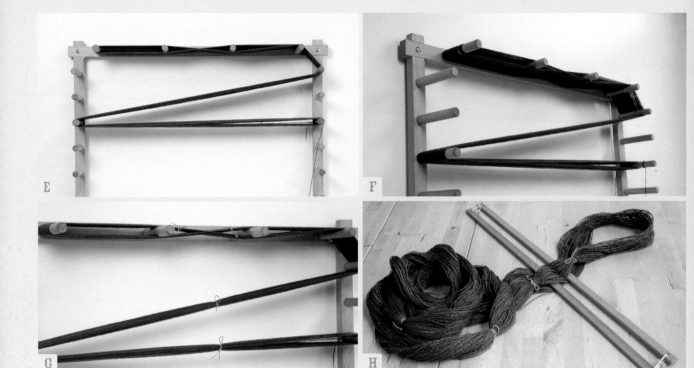

6. Continue wrapping the yarn so it goes over the rightmost peg on the horizontal part of the frame and then down the warping board, following the existing path of yarn. **[E]**

7. Continue wrapping the yarn, following the previous wraps as many times as needed to complete 1 inch (2.5 cm) of warp. For instance if the E.P.I. (see page 79) is 12, then you need to wrap up and down the board 12 times. Tie a piece of string through the cross (at the top of the frame), grouping the 12 ends in your first inch, together. This way you can keep count while warping. **[F]**

8. When you have completed winding the warp, place choke ties at 1-yard (0.9 m) intervals, between pegs. This will help to keep the warp from tangling when you remove it from the warping board. **[G]**

9. Tie strings around the cross (step 5) to keep it clearly marked, making it easier to insert the lease sticks.

10. With the warp still on the board, insert lease sticks through the cross (step 5), one on each side. Tie the ends of the lease sticks together with about 1 inch (2.5 cm) of space between them. The warp and the lease sticks should be at perpendicular angles when you look at them. On one side of the lease sticks is the short loop where you turned around every time you reached the top of the warping board. On the other side of the lease sticks is the long stretch of warp. **[H]**

## Removing the Warp from the Board

If you have tied marking strings throughout the warp and around the cross, you can remove it from the board. However, it's less likely to tangle if you chain the warp. Chaining is a simple way to keep the strings organized before you start dressing the loom, by creating a sort of looped braid.

11. Starting at the bottom (or top) of the board, place your hand through the loop around the last peg. Slowly remove it, making sure the rest of the warp stays on the board. (Or if the warp isn't too long, you can take it all off and chain it as shown here.)

12. With the loop in one hand, insert your other hand through the loop and grab the warp just above (or below). Pull the warp through the loop to form a new loop. **[A, B, C]**

13. Twist your hand, put it back through the loop, and grab the next bit of warp, and pull it through the loop to form a new loop. Repeat this until you get to the end of the warp. This keeps the yarn bundle organized. **[D, E, F]**

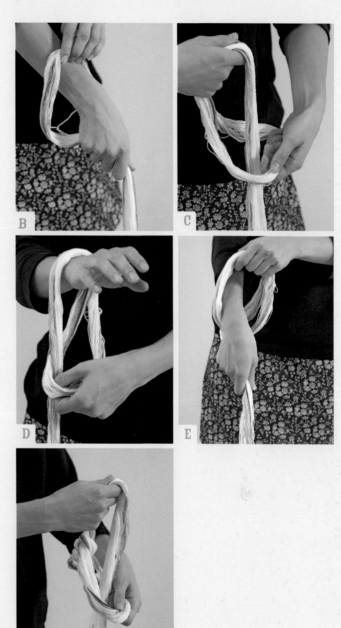

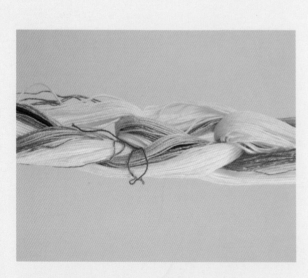

This is an example of chaining in basic crochet stitch, which helps to keep your warp threads organized and untangled before moving it to the loom for dressing.

# Dressing the Loom

Dressing the loom is next in the weaving process, and it includes many steps. It is important to take your time and finish each step correctly. It is easy to make mistakes, so be patient and work slowly. If you can't sit for long periods of time, take breaks. Sometimes it helps to dress the loom with a partner so you can finish faster and get weaving sooner.

- Winding warp onto the back beam

- Threading the heddles according to the pattern

- Sleying or threading the reed to disperse threads evenly across the warp

- Tying on to the front beam to create tension in the warp from front to back

- Tying up the treadles to raise the right combination of harnesses, according to the pattern

## Beaming the Warp

The first step in dressing the loom in preparation of weaving is connecting one end of the warp to the back, or warp beam. You then wind it onto the beam, using the lease sticks and the cross to help organize and untangle the threads as they go on the beam.

14. First, be sure that you have ties securing the ends of each lease stick together so that there is no way that the warp could slide off. Standing at the back of your loom, place the long chained section of warp through the heddles so the bundle rests facing the front of the loom. You will be tying the lease sticks between the castle (which encases the harnesses) and the back beam. The chained warp should go toward the direction of the front of the loom so that you can dress the loom from the front once your warp has been wound onto the back beam.

15. Cut four long pieces of strong cord or yarn. Tie one length of cord or yarn to each of the four holes in the lease stick so that you can attach one lease stick to the castle and one to the back of the loom so that the lease sticks holding the end of your warp are suspended. The small loop of the warp should be towards the back beam. The lease sticks should hang in the center of the harnesses or lower. **[A]**

A

Your lease sticks should be tied to the back beam and the castle so they float between and will hold up your cross while you wind your warp onto the warp beam.

16. Thread the warp beam rod through the small loop in the warp that is facing the back of the loom. It is very important that you connect the warp to the rod over the back beam. Remove the choke ties around the cross, the counting threads, and the two ties closest to the cross. Spread out the loop so that it is as wide as the project. **[B, C, D]**

17. Move to the front of the loom and smooth the warp with your fingers. If you are working alone, loosely tie the smoothed and spread out warp around the beater, making sure the beater is leaning on the front beam. If you have a partner, he or she can hold the warp in the front.

18. Walk to the back of the loom and slowly use the crank to wind the warp onto the warp beam. Make sure that the gears in the front are engaged and that warp stays spread out to the desired width as it winds on the warp beam. After one full rotation of the warp around the warp beam, insert a sheet of stiff paper between the layers of warp. If you have the coordination, keep the warp beam brake released while beaming the warp so as not to wear out the break. If you are working with a partner, have him or her depress the brake while you crank and insert paper. **[E, F]**

19. Continue this process, smoothing the warp as needed, until you have about 2 feet (0.6 m) of unwound warp left. When you reach this point, cut the ends at the unwound end of the warp to get rid of the remaining loop and tangle.

20. Move the cords from the front lease stick to the back one so that the warp waterfalls from the lease sticks down the back of the harnesses. Do not take out the lease sticks yet! **[G]**

## Threading the Heddles

This step is the first in setting up the structure of the fabric; it is when you decide and prepare for patterning. For this tutorial, we are using a 4-harness loom and a 1, 2, 3, 4 pattern.

21. Sit at the front of the loom. All the yarns should be flowing over the lease sticks, after being wound on the warp beam. Slide all of the heddles to the left.

22. Start by separating one heddle from every harness and move them to the right. The harnesses are numbered from 1 to 4 on this style loom. **[A]**

23. Thread the first warp yarn (the rightmost thread in the lease sticks) through the eye of the heddle on the fourth harness using a long threading hook. **[B]**

24. Thread the second warp yarn, or warp end, (the second thread from the right in the lease sticks) through the heddle on the third harness.

25. Thread the third yarn from the right through the heddle on the second harness.

26. Thread the fourth yarn from the right through the heddle on the first harness. **[C]**

27. Tie the threads going through the first group of heddles into a loose slipknot so they don't slip back out of the heddles as you are working. **[D]**

28. Separate one heddle from every harness and continue threading in the same order as the threads are arranged in the cross. This kind of threading (1, 2, 3, 4/1, 2, 3, 4) is a called a straight draw.

29. Repeat until you run out of warp yarns (ends) and remember to tie bundles together as you go so you do not accidentally undo your hard work.

Shown here is a floating selvage, which always floats in the middle of the open shed because it is not threaded through any heddle and will never be raised or lowered.

# FLOATING SELVAGE

Woven fabrics have finished side edges called selvages; however, hand-woven fabrics often have irregular selvages because every few picks the yarn is not caught into the weave. This happens because some weave structures (such as twills) are dependent on the same harnesses being raised several times in a row, which means that those ends are not being woven into the cloth. The result looks like an error because the rightmost and leftmost threads in the warp float along the edge of the cloth. There are a couple of things you can do to ensure parallel and neat edges: one is to manually anchor the weft into the warp, and the other is to create floating selvages.

To manually anchor this outermost thread, insert the shuttle around the last end in the warp whenever it doesn't catch automatically. You may need to weave a bit to notice where and when to manually wrap the weft around the outermost thread if it is not being raised.

Floating selvedges take a bit of planning and can be used with any warp. Some weavers always use a floating selvedge regardless of the pattern being woven because it is a simple way to ensure neat edges. Once you are ready to tie the warp onto the loom, you'll need to unthread the first and last warp ends from the heddles they are threaded through. The two loose threads should be sleyed through the reed and tied on with the rest of the warp, without going through any heddle, so that when you raise harnesses, they will stay stationary. Because the first and last thread (leftmost and rightmost threads) are not threaded through a heddle, they will float above the rest of the warp ends when the harnesses are not being raised. When the shed is opened, the warp ends in the raised harnesses will be higher than the first and last thread so that those will float across the middle of the shed. Usually, having threads in the shed is not a positive thing because they will snag the weft, but here that is their express purpose. To weave, always enter the shed over the floating selvedge and always exit the shed under the floating selvedge on the other side. The angle of entry and exit from the shed feels natural, so this action becomes automatic and requires no more thought than weaving without floating selvedges.

## Sleying the Reed

Also called threading the reed, this next step further organizes the threads by putting them through the reed. The reed is what separates the threads and distributes them evenly across the loom. Each slot in the reed is called a "dent" (refer to dents per inch on page 77).

30. Finally, you can remove the lease sticks from the warp. Sit at the front of the loom so you can see the tied bunches threaded through the heddles. Separate the heddles down the middle, moving half to the left and half to the right. **[A]**

31. Stabilize the beater in the upright position (some looms have a tool that keeps the beater from moving).

32. Measure and make note of the center of the reed. For a 1, 2, 3, 4 pattern, follow the steps below. If you are weaving with more harnesses, adjust accordingly.

33. Untie the slipknot in the first group of four yarns on the left-hand side of the heddle divide closest to the center.

34. Thread (or sley) the yarn end threaded through the heddle on the fourth harness through the center-most dent in the reed.

35. Thread (or sley) the yarn end threaded through the heddle on the third harness through the dent to the left of the first threaded dent.

36. Thread (or sley) the yarn end threaded through the heddle on the second harness through the dent to the left of the second threaded dent.

37. Thread (or sley) the yarn end threaded through the heddle on the first harness through the dent to the left of the third threaded dent.

38. Repeat until you run out of yarn ends to the left of the center. Tie bunches of threads together every ten dents or so. This way, you won't lose the work you've done. **[B, C]**

39. Thread the other half of the warp from the center out and continue as for the first half (steps 34–39) until you run out of yarn ends.

A

B

C

## TIP — Density Stripes

You can create density stripes in your warp while you are sleying the reed. Try threading ten dents with one thread and then the successive ten dents with two threads per dent. This will make your fabric denser in the places with two through the reed and is a subtle way to create variation. Try different density stripes!

## Tying On

Use a series of Larks Head Knots (see page 91) to secure the warp to the front of the loom (with an apron stick attached to the cloth beam) and adjust the tension before you start weaving. It is very important that the warp tension is even across the warp or the woven fabric could have a visible waved edge.

**40.** Untie the groups of yarn in the reed. Hold all the warp yarns together and press the brake pedal (usually to the right of the treadles), pulling enough warp forward off the warp beam so that the yarns don't fall back through the reed, and that you have enough room to tie the bows.

**41.** Divide the warp in half and work from the center outwards. As a general guideline, tie on groups or bunches of yarn about 1 inch (2.5 cm) wide. If you are using a 12 dent reed, for example, bunch 12 yarns together since there are 12 dents in 1 inch (2.5 cm). As you tie the yarns onto the front of the loom, tie a bunch from the left, then the right, then left, and so on until all the yarns are tied on. This ensures that you are tying on evenly. Secure the bunches with Larks Head Knots (see 90).

**42.** It is better to secure the yarns with bows rather than knots because it is easier to go back and adjust bows. As you are working across the warp, tying it on, check the tension by patting and moving your hand on top of the warp from left to right. Does it feel even? You will be able to tell which bunches feel looser than others, and generally as you continue to tie on, the middle knots start to loosen. If you've used bows, you can easily go back to the knots that need some tightening.

**43.** Once it feels like there is even tension across the warp, you're ready to weave! Take the time to make sure the tension is even because you will not be able to adjust tension in your warp again until you cut your project off the loom and tie back on.

After you have tied on your warps to the front beam apron stick with larks head knots, you are ready to weave, starting with a header. The header is the first several inches of weaving that even out your warp from left to right. Using paper toweling or tissue makes this faster.

## Tie Up

Before you start weaving, there is one last step. At this point, you need to tie up the harnesses to the treadles. Because weaving involves raising and lowering harnesses, which in turn raise or lower the threads attached to them, you have to do this in the desired order to create a pattern. The order is dictated by the draft (pattern) you have chosen. Following your chosen draft, connect each harness to a specific treadle on the floor, so that when you push on each treadle, you actually lift the harness to which it is attached, raising the threads to create the shed for the shuttle to pass through.

For example, to execute a plain weave, which raises every other thread, you use just two treadles on a 4-harness loom. Attach harnesses 1 and 3 to one treadle, and harnesses 2 and 4 to another. This way, as you alternate treadles, you are raising every other thread.

The tie-up will change with every pattern, so see the section on basic draft reading (page 96).

# Tie a Larks Head Knot

The Larks Head Knot allows you to adjust the tension of the warp while tying on. As you tie the warp to the front of the loom, you will be able to come back and untie the knots to readjust the tension across the warp. As you tie each bunch, try to keep the tension uniform and avoid tying each successive knot tighter or the middle bunches will become very loose.

1. Separate about 12 warp yarns from the reed and hold them taut over the apron stick.

2. Wrap the yarns over the top of the stick and then under, maintaining the tension. Divide the strings in half under the stick and wrap each half in opposite directions up and around the warp threads on top of the stick and tie a single knot. **[A, B, C]**

3. Holding one half of the tie in one hand and the other bunch in the other hand, tug them forward and away from the back beam, so you are creating the tension you need. **[D]**

4. Pull the divided parts back toward you and up so that you don't lose the tension. Tie the first part of a regular knot (over and under) and then tie a second knot or a bow. **[E]**

5. Repeat across the warp with all the yarns. **[F]**

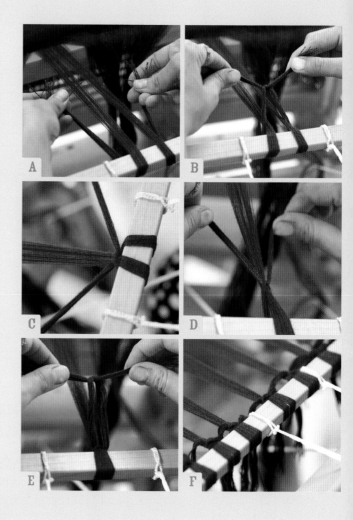

## Correcting Errors

Before you start weaving, you'll want to check that the warp is tied on correctly and the harnesses are tied as needed to weave the desired pattern (page 96). Raise each harness independently and peer through the shed (the opening between the top and bottom threads). If there are any thread crossings, you have made a threading error and should fix it at this point. It will not correct itself and will only continue to bother you and interfere with the pattern.

To fix a threading error, untie the Larks Head Knot that corresponds to the offending warp thread. Release the offending warp end and follow it through the reed to the heddles.

- In the best case scenario, the threads are crossed between the heddles and the reed, and you can just switch the crossed threads in the reed.

- If you have threaded two threads through two heddles on the same harness, you can make a fake heddle using wire or thread on the harness where the end should have been. Then you can thread one of the warp through the fake heddle and back into the reed.

- If you have skipped a heddle, your task is harder. You can pull out the warp bundle with the missing end and rethread the reed from that point to the opposite side of the bundle to close the gap. Or you may unthread the heddles and reed from the error out to the opposite side of the entire warp and rethread correctly.

## How to Create a Fake Heddle

Threading errors are inevitable. Some you can fix and others you can't, but if you've forgotten to thread one end, you can create a fake heddle so that you don't have to undo all the tying on. As you'll find out, setting up is a tedious process, with a big reward once you are weaving. You'll want to know this trick!

1. Measure the length of the heddles.

2. Collect a length of twine or strong cotton yarn that doesn't break easily and cut it twice the length of the heddle, plus several inches. **[A]**

3. Fold the twine in half. Find the place in the warp threading order where you need the heddle and put the folded end of the twine over the top of the harness at the location. Wrap it over the bar and pull the ends through the loop so it is connected to the top of the heddle bar. **[B]**

4. Run your hand down the heddle to find where the top of the eye of the heddles next to it are. Tie a knot here. **[C]**

5. Drop down about half an inch (1 cm) and tie another knot. You've now created an eye to thread your missing warp end through. **[D]**

6. Tie the thread to the bottom heddle bar, keeping your fake heddle taut.

7. Thread the missing warp thread through the eye, and *voila!* **[E]**

# Winding a Bobbin

Once the loom is set and dressed correctly, you need to prepare the weft before you weave. This involves winding a bobbin of weft thread to insert into the shuttle. It is very helpful to have a bobbin winder.

1. Attach the bobbin winder to a counter or table and secure an empty bobbin in it. Place the yarn on the floor below the table so it unwinds easily.

2. Wrap the loose end of the yarn tightly around the bobbin several times. Twist the yarn ends together so that the ply meets the bobbin.

3. Turn the handle on the bobbin winder to wind the yarn onto the bobbin. Hold the yarn in your other hand with enough tension to wind tightly onto the bobbin. As you wind, direct the yarn from left to right so it builds up evenly across the bobbin. **[A]**

4. When the bobbin is full, cut the yarn and insert the wound bobbin onto the shuttle. Pull the yarn through the hole in the front of the shuttle, and you are ready to weave. You might want to make extra bobbins so you don't have to stop weaving to wind a new one. **[B]**

A

B

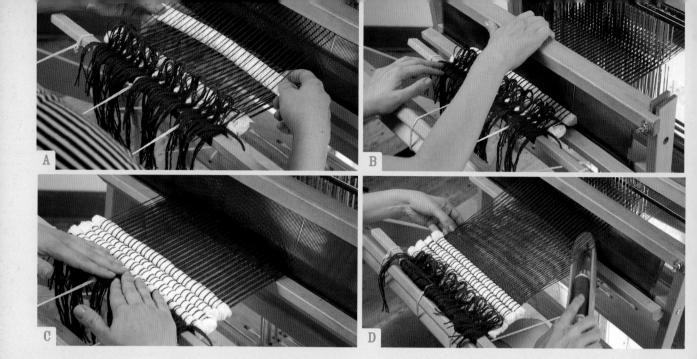

A B C D

# WEAVING

Once you've dressed the loom you can begin. Weaving itself is a series of steps done over and over to build the fabric thread by thread.

1. Weave a few inches, (referred to as the header), to even out the warp and eliminate the triangular spaces created during tying on. The header won't be used as part of the finished woven cloth. Speed up the process by using a paper towel as weft because it is thick and will weave the header faster than thin thread. Weave the header the same as the rest of the cloth by raising harnesses, placing a strip of paper towel through the shed, beating, switching harnesses, and repeating.
   **[A, B, C]**

2. Press down on the first treadle indicated in the pattern. Holding the shuttle in one hand, pass it through the shed to the other side. Hold the tail end of the yarn so it doesn't pull through.

3. Release the treadle and pull the beater toward you to pack the weft yarn into place. Beating affects the density of the cloth; if you beat hard, the yarns will pack tightly, making a denser fabric.

4. Press the next treadle in the pattern and pass the shuttle back through the newly formed shed in the opposite direction. Again, release the treadle and beat the yarn. To weave, simply repeat! **[D]**

5. Follow the draft (pattern). As you weave, you'll notice that you are building up fabric, and that the shed is getting smaller. Periodically, you'll need to advance the warp, moving the woven fabric forward and onto the cloth (front) beam. To do this, release the brake and wind the cloth onto the cloth beam using your hand to rotate the cloth beam or use the crank on the outside of the frame.

6. Once you have woven the desired length, you can release the brake and cut the project from the loom. Release enough warp from the back to pull forward a bit and cut across the warp while holding the warp threads close to the reed. Leave enough warp length between the fabric and the cutting location to allow for fringe, if desired. This only applies if you still have warp on your loom that you want to weave. If you are finished weaving the warp, you can let it fall through the reed. Unroll and remove the fabric from the front beam and untie the fabric from the apron stick. If you have more warp on the loom, tie a quick knot in front of the reed so that the threads do not fall through.

## TIP  Tension Too Loose?

If at anytime during weaving, the tension seems loose and uneven, you can cut off your fabric and tie the warp back on to the front. You will, however, lose some warp length by doing this since each time you tie on to the front beam it uses at least 6 inches (15.2 cm) of warp.

## FINISHING

After you have woven the last pick in your cloth, you are ready to start the finishing process. This can be as simple as cutting the cloth off the loom, tying a few knots to secure the weft into place, and giving it a gentle wash by hand. It can also be a highly involved process of decoration and ornamentation and chemical treatments.

## TWINING

Twining is a way of finishing the fabric on the loom, eliminating the need to hem it once it is off the loom. Twining involves twisting a piece of yarn around each individual warp thread to prevent the weft from coming undone once the warp is cut from the loom.

1. Cut a length of yarn (warp, weft, or even a different color yarn) several times the width of the warp.

2. Fold the twining yarn in half to mark the midpoint.

3. Position the twining yarn so the midpoint wraps around the outermost (selvage) wrap yarn, close to the last shot (shuttle passage). Cross the ends of the yarn to create one twist between the warp yarns. Wrap and twist the yarn around the next warp yarn to create a second twist. Continue this way across the warp. Tie a knot at the end to prevent unraveling.

## MAKING TASSELS

Winding tassels is a great, decorative way to finish any woven cloth. You will need a tassel winder, which usually comes with several pinchers, to grab the yarns.

1. Decide how many warp yarns you want for each tassel and separate the desired number.

2. Divide the yarns in half and attach one half to one pincher and the other half to the pincher next to it. Turn the tassel winder clockwise to twist the yarns in one direction, twisting until they are about to buckle onto themselves.

3. Release the two sections from the pinchers, holding them so they don't untwist. Attach both to one pincher.

4. Turn the tassel winder counterclockwise to twist the sections together so they wrap onto each other. Continue until they are about to buckle.

5. Release the pincher and tie a knot at the end of the twisted yarns. Continue across the width of the warp.

## SEWING

If you do not want to twine or have fringe, you can sew the ends of cloth. Hand-sew a straight or blanket stitch or machine stitch a straight or zigzag stitch across the cut ends. The ends will still be raw, however, so if you prefer a very clean finish, hem the fabric.

## Reading a Weaving Draft

The draft is most easily described as a rectangular diagram with four quadrants. It shows a picture of the pattern to be woven and instructs the weaver how to thread the loom, tie up the harnesses, and in what order to treadle to create the pattern shown. Once you are comfortable dressing the loom, you should explore the many fascinating and beautiful patterns available for the home weaver. Understanding and being able to read a draft will open up endless possibilities of weaving and designing your own patterns. We are particularly in love with *Handweaver's Pattern Directory* by Anne Dixon.

## DRAW-DOWN

The draw-down is a graphic representation of the woven cloth that provides an idea of the patterning that a particular draft produces. Sometimes this image is a photograph of a finished sample. Most of the time, however, the image is a black and white graphic. It looks pixilated because it is a representation of the grid created by the interlacing of the warp and the weft. It does not show any texturing effects or dimensionality, so proceed with caution when choosing yarn. For help choosing the appropriate yarn look for the designer's notes on the suggested yarn weight somewhere on the top, bottom, or margin of the page.

In order to program your loom to create the patterns you would like, you use a pattern draft. This chart gives all the basic information on how to thread and treadle your loom. Shown here is a basic pattern draft for a 2/2 twill–a widely used weave structure.

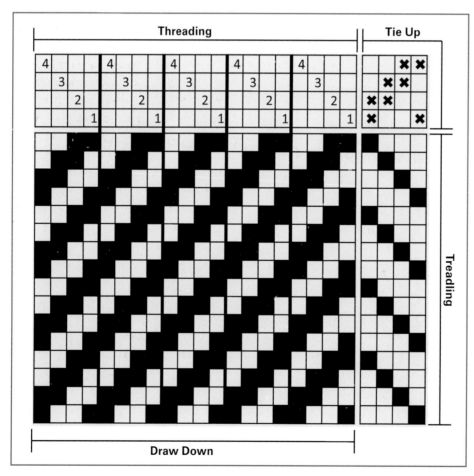

## Threading

The top-left quadrant is dedicated to threading and shows one repeat of the pattern. The markings can be Xs, diamonds, dots, or numbers, all indicating a threaded heddle. A repeat can be as short as two warp ends or so long that it requires several lines. The threading may be read left to right or right to left depending on the designer and the publication; the correct direction will usually be indicated in the draft.

In the case of a four-harness loom, the threading consists of four rows and a sequence of markings distributed throughout them. A marking in the first row from the bottom, followed by a marking in the second row, a marking in the third, and a marking in the fourth, indicate that the loom should be threaded in a straight draw. A straight draw is the simplest threading sequence with warp ends threaded one per harness, in a 1, 2, 3, 4 order. If the threading is 1, 2, 3, 4, it will have only the four markings displayed in the draft.

## Tie-up

The top-right quadrant in the draft is the tie-up. This explains which harnesses should be tied up together and to which treadle. The four rows that represent the four harnesses in the threading section are the same four rows in the tie-up, but the new vertical columns represent the treadles.

The draft may show different markings in the tie-up section. Xs indicate a sinking shed such as those found on countermarch or counterbalance looms, and Os indicate a rising shed, such as the ones on jack-type looms. If the draft is written for a countermarch loom and you have a jack loom, invert the tie-up by inserting Os into the blank spaces and ignoring the Xs. For example, if the draft indicates to tie up harnesses 1 and 2 to the first treadle on a sinking shed loom, you should tie up harnesses 3 and 4 to the first treadle on a rising shed loom to achieve the same result.

The way the harnesses are tied up to the treadles depends on the loom type. The ties can be made of natural rope or string, nylon cords, or metal wires or chains. In some cases, table looms and smaller floor looms (with four or less harnesses) are permanently tied up in a direct tie-up. A loom with more than four harnesses is never permanently tied up because it is not humanly possible to raise harness 1, 3, and 5, for example, with two feet.

The simplest tie-up, called the direct tie-up, connects the first harness to the left most treadle, the second harness to the second treadle from the left, the third harness to the third treadle from the left, and the fourth harness to the fourth treadle from the left. If this is the tie-up being used, the tie-up quadrant of the draft may be left blank.

## TREADLING

The treadling section of the draft indicates the order to raise the harnesses for each pick (passage of the shuttle). It is usually read from the top down, but sometimes from the bottom up to simulate the weaving process. If you have a table loom or another loom that is tied up in a direct tie-up formation, each row will show the harness or harnesses that need to be raised. Each column represents one harness; the first column represents the first harness, the second column the second harness, and so on. If harness 1 and 2 need to be raised at the same time, that row will show the first and second box marked. If you have a direct tie-up loom, it might be easier to rewrite the treadling sequence in numerical form.

If your loom is tied up with multiple harnesses per treadle, the treadling section will tell you the order to depress the treadles, rather than raise the harnesses. If you have finished the tie-up, all you have to do is follow the sequence, reading each row and throwing, or passing, the shuttle through the shed.

If you are weaving with different weft yarns, this section indicates, usually with different capital letters, when to weave which weft. An *A* in the first row followed by a *B* in the second, and an *A* in the third, and a *B* in the fourth, is telling the weaver to alternate the weft for each shot. If the treadling instructions also indicate numbers, then the shuttle must be thrown that many times through the shed. If both color and the number of throws of the shuttle per shed must be noted, then colored ink might be used to indicate weft color, with a number printed in the middle.

The creative potential of working on a loom is endless. There are books devoted entirely to the weaving process and amazing patterns that provide direction and step-by-step instruction. Once you have learned to dress your loom and have practiced basic weaving technique, you'll certainly want to experiment with more advanced projects.

Shown here is the process of double width to create a blanket that is twice the width of the weaving width on the loom. This is done by weaving two layers on top of one another at the same time, connected on one side so that the cloth can be opened when it is taken off the loom.

## Double Cloth + Double Width

There are many ways you can advance your weaving techniques once you feel comfortable with your loom and the process. Aside from advanced patterns and learning to draft your own patterns, you can also create double cloth and double width fabrics. For example, if you would like to make coverlets, curtains, or a tablecloth, you don't need a bigger loom—you only need to know how to weave double cloth.

Weaving double cloth is a technique that allows you to make two or more layers of cloth at the same time. The only requirement for double cloth is a loom with a minimum of four harnesses because each layer requires at least two (for which you can use plain weave). You are able to weave two layers on top of one another. If your loom has more than four, you will be able to weave layers with more complex patterns or weave more layers with simpler patterns.

In double width cloth, you are connecting the layers while you weave. Connecting the layers on one side or two sides opens up a variety of possibilities. As the name suggests, this is a way to weave cloth that is at least twice as wide as the natural weaving width of the loom. If the layers of cloth are woven in a certain sequence, with the same shuttle, they will be connected on one selvage to create connected layers. When the cloth is cut off the loom, it will unfold into a single cloth at least twice the weaving width of the loom.

If two layers are connected at both selvages, the finished cloth forms a tube. Weaving tubes may seem like a novelty compared to the obvious practicality of weaving double-wide cloth, but consider the time saved sewing the cloth into pillows or totes. With the sides closed, there is no finishing to be done off the loom.

# Simple Woven Placemats

The best way to learn how to weave is through practice! This project is shown on a standard, 4-harness floor loom, can be adapted to other looms. Weaving fringed placemats on one warp, with a plain weave pattern, is a fun and practical project.

## PLANNING

For this project, we've plugged the correct numbers into the formulas on page 80 to make four placemats that are each 14 x 18 inches (35.6 x 45.7 cm).

A finished, woven placemat makes a great addition to your table. This project is quick to weave once you've set up your loom and requires little finishing.

## DETERMINING THE AMOUNT OF WARP YARN NEEDED

1. **Length of one warp**

| | | |
|---|---|---|
| Desired length for 4 placemats, each 18" (45.7 cm) long | = | 72" (1,8 m) |
| Fringe length, 8" (20.3 cm) per placemat (4" [10.2 cm] each side) | = | 32" (81.3 cm) |
| Take-up (page 77) | = | 11" (27.9 cm) |
| Shrinkage, approximately 10% | = | 11" (27.9 cm) |
| Loom waste (about one yard [0.9 m]) | = | 36" (91.4 cm) |
| **= Total length of warp needed** | = | **162" or 4.5 yards (4.1 m)** |

**Note:** You'll need to know when to stop and start weaving each individual placemat so they are each 18 inches (45.7 cm) long (but will have the desired length of warp for fringe) when taken off the loom and washed. To determine this number, apply the formula above using 18 inches (45.7 cm) as the desired length of project and exclude the fringe length.

So the math should read as follows: 18 + 2+ 2= 22 inches (55.9 cm). This is the length you need to weave for each placemat, before you stop weaving to allow for fringe.

## DETERMINING THE WIDTH OF WARP YARN NEEDED

2. **Width of warp**

| | | |
|---|---|---|
| Desired finished width of project | = | 14" (35.6 cm) |
| Draw-in (page 77) | = | 2" (5.1 cm) |
| Shrinkage, approximately 10% | = | 6" (15.2 cm) |
| **= Warp width on loom** | = | **22" (55.9 cm)** |

3. **total number of ends needed**

| | | |
|---|---|---|
| Warp width on loom (as determined by formula 2) | = | 22" (55.9 cm) |
| x Warp sett (E.P.I.) | = | x 12 E.P.I |
| **= Total ends needed** | = | **264 ends** |

4. **Total yardage of warp yarn needed**

| | | |
|---|---|---|
| Total ends needed (as determined by formula 3) | = | 264 ends |
| x total length of one wrap needed (as determined by formula 1) | = | x 162" (4.1 m) |
| **= Total warp yardage** | = | **42,768", or 1,188 yards (1,069 m)** |

## DETERMINING THE AMOUNT OF WEFT YARN NEEDED

1. **Total yardage of weft yarn**

| | | |
|---|---|---|
| Length of one weft shot (as determined by formula 2) | = | 22" (55.9 cm) |
| x Picks per inch or (P.P.I) * | = | x 12 |
| **= Amount needed to weave 1" (2.5 cm) of fabric** | = | **264" (6.7 m)** |

2. **Amount needed to weave 1" (2.5 cm) of fabric**

| | | |
|---|---|---|
| | = | **264" (6.7 m)** |
| x desired length (excluding fringe) | = | x 72" (182.9 cm) |
| **= Total weft yardage** | = | **19,008", or 528 yards (475 m)** |

*If the same fiber is used for warp and weft, the P.P.I. is the same as E.P.I.

## WINDING THE WARP

This project requires a 4½-yard (4.1 m)-long warp, so round up to 5 yards (4.6 m). Refer to the step-by-step tutorial (page 82) for more in depth instruction.

1. Prepare your yarn by placing it in a basket or between your feet so you can unwind it easily without it rolling away. Tie the end of the yarn to the third peg from the top on the right.

2. Using your dominant hand, trail the yarn across the warping board and around the opposite left peg. Travel back to the right side and around the peg above the first peg where the yarn is tied. Continue for a total of five times, including across the top of the board. Make sure to form a cross (page 82) in the center, across the top of the board. There should be a length of 5 yards (4.6 m) on the board.

3. Reverse direction of the yarn, following the trail of wraps as many times as needed to complete 1 inch (2.5 cm) of warp, in this case 12 (E.P.I.). Tie a

piece of string through the cross (at the top of the frame), grouping the 12 ends in your first inch. This way you can keep count while warping.

4. When you have completed winding the warp, place choke ties at 1-yard (0.9 m) intervals, between pegs. This will help to keep the warp from tangling when you remove it from the warping board. Tie strings around the cross to keep it clearly marked, making it easier to insert the lease sticks.

5. Remove the warp from the board by chaining it (page 83).

## DRESSING THE LOOM: BEAMING THE WARP

Refer to the detailed instructions for beaming the warp on page 84.

6. Position the warp in the loom by tying the lease sticks to the castle. Thread the warp beam rod through the small loop in the warp. Remove the choke ties and smooth out the loop so it is as wide as the project, in this case 17 inches (43.2 cm).

7. Loosely tie the spread out warp around the beater and make sure the beater is leaning on the front beam. From the back of the loom, slowly use the crank to wind the warp on the warp beam. Add a sheet of paper between each full rotation.

8. Continue cranking and winding the warp onto the beam until there is about 2 feet (0.6 m) of unwound warp remaining. Cut the loop of unwound warp. Move the cords from the front lease stick to the back one so the warp waterfalls down the back of the harnesses. Leave the lease sticks in place.

## Dressing the Loom: Threading the Heddles

Refer to the detailed instructions for threading the heddles on page 86.

9. Sit at the front of the loom with all yarns flowing over the lease sticks and the heddles gathered to the left of the loom. Separate one heddle from each harness, moving them to the right.

10. Thread the first warp through the heddle on the fourth harness using a threading hook. Thread the second warp yarn through the heddle on the third harness. And so on. Once the first four heddles are threaded, tie them together in a loose slipknot.

11. Continue in the same 1, 2, 3, 4/1, 2, 3, 4 pattern until you run out of warp yarns. This threading is called a straight draw. Remember to tie the bundles of four yarns together.

## Dressing the Loom: Sleying the Reed

Refer to the detailed instructions for sleying the reed on page 88.

12. Remove the lease sticks from the warp and separate the heddles down the middle, moving half to the left and half to the right. Stabilize the beater.

13. Untie the slipknot in the first group of four yarns on the left-hand side of the heddle divide closest to the center. Sley the yarn end threaded through the heddle on the fourth harness through the centermost dent in the reed. Sley the yarn end threaded through the heddle on the third harness through the dent to the left of the first threaded dent. Continue in the same manner until the first four yarn ends are threaded.

14. Continue until all the yarn ends to the left of the center are threaded, tying bunches every ten dents. Repeat with all the yarn ends to the right side of the heddle divide.

## Dressing the Loom: Tying On

Refer to the detailed instructions for tying on page 89.

15. Untie the bunches of yarn in the reed and press the brake pedal, pulling the warp forward so you have room to tie the warp to the front beam. Divide the warp in half and work from the center outwards, tying bunches of about 12 yarns to the front of the loom, securing them with Larks Head Knots (page 90). Tie a bunch to the left of the center and then to the right all the way across the warp.

16. Make sure the tension of the warp is even and slightly taut. Smooth your hand over the yarns to make sure they feel even. Adjust the knots as needed.

## Dressing the Loom: Tie Up

**Plain weave:** You can choose any pattern or weave for your placemats, but the most simple is the plain weave, which uses a direct tie-up (see page 89). To execute a plain weave, which raises every other thread, you use just two treadles on a 4-harness loom. Attach harnesses 1 and 3 to one treadle and harnesses 2 and 4 to another. This way, as you alternate treadles, you are raising every other thread.

**Twill weave:** For the placemats shown, we used a 2/2 twill pattern. You can refer to the twill draft at the very beginning of the draft reading section (page 96). Twills are one of the very basic weave structures. There is a 1/3 twill (where 1 harness is raised at a time), 2/2 twill (where every combination of two harnesses are raised at a time), and a 3/1 twill (where three harnesses are raised at a time). To tie up for a 2/2 twill, you can do a direct tie-up (where one harness is attached to one treadle, so that you can raise each individually). Then your treadling will be harness 1+2 together, then 2+3, then 3+4, then 4+1, and so on.

**You can also tie up as follows:** Harness 1+2 on treadle 1; harness 2+3 on treadle 2; harnesses 3+4 on treadle 3; and harnesses 4+1 on treadle 4. This way, you only need to press one treadle per weft shot. Please refer to the section on reading and understanding drafts.

## WEAVING & FINISHING

Before you start weaving you should check for any dressing errors (page 91) and wind several bobbins (page 93).

You'll be weaving four placemats, each with fringe. Remember that the formulas indicated the need to allow 4 inches (10.2 cm) for fringe, then weave 22 inches (55.9 cm) and then allow 8 inches (20.3 cm) again for 4 inches (10.2 cm) + 4 inches (10.2 cm) of fringe (the end of one placemat and the beginning of the other) and so on to finish the four placemats. It is important to weave paper towels, the same as if they were weft yarn, to act as space holders for the fringe.

17. Weave header to even out warp using paper towels or toilet paper. Allow for 4 inches (10.2 cm) of fringe here, at least. After the fringe, weave one row of a twining border (page 95).

18. Start weaving the first placemat, following a twill pattern, shown by the draft. Refer to the section on draft reading (page 96) to better understand the draft. If you have done a tie-up for 2/2 twill, your treadling will be 1, 2, 3, 4/1, 2, 3, 4 and so on. If you have done a direct tie up, you will need to hold down two treadles at once in the following sequence: 1+2, 2+3, 3+4, 4+1 and repeat.

19. Once you have woven 22 inches (55.9 cm), weave another twining border to finish the first placemat. Weave 8 inches (20.3 cm) of paper towels as a place holder for fringe (4 inches [10.2 cm] for the first placemat and 4 inches [10.2 cm] for the second, as you will cut through the middle to separate your placemats once they are all woven). After

weaving 8 inches (20.3 cm) of paper towels or toilet paper, twine another row to start the second placemat and weave another 22 inches (55.9 cm), the same as for the first placemat. Finish with a twining border and repeat the entire sequence for two more placemats, so you have four in total.

20. When you've finished the last placemat with a twining border, cut all of your work from the loom. Release the brake and pull from the warp beam. Holding the warp in one hand, cut across the warp. Unroll the weaving from the cloth beam and untie the fabric from the apron stick.

21. Lay out the weaving on a flat surface and using sharp scissors, cut across the warp in the middle of the fringe between placemats so there is 4 inches (10.2 cm) at each end of each placemat. Remove all the paper towel or toilet paper from the fringe. You can trim the fringe short, if you wish, or you can hem the ends.

22. Finally, handwash the placemats gently in luke-warm water with a little bit of soap. Rinse and lay them out to dry.

---

TIP  **Creating Zigzag**

Here we have done a 2/2 twill with a directional change. This means that we did a treadling of 1, 2, 3, 4 a few times and then went back the other way for a few repeats, which changes the direction of the twill. Feel free to play around with this idea!

# Printing

**Printmaking is the process by which an artist creates multiple copies of the exact same image.** Though most printmaking processes can be used to print on fabric, those most commonly used to create beautiful textiles, now and throughout history, are screen printing and block printing. Fortunately, both of these printmaking techniques are easily done in a home studio. Artists and fabric designers use both methods to create one-off prints, full editions (a set of prints that are exact replications), or repeat patterns for yardage.

Both block and screen printing can be used to create simple or highly intricate patterns and imagery on paper, fabric, and other surfaces. Single color images are very simple to print, while images with multiple colors require a few additional steps. Multiple color images need to be separated into individual layers for each color and then each layer must be applied on top of each other. Each layer utilizes some method of registration so the multiple layers are aligned perfectly so the printed images aren't blurry. There are several registration methods (see page 106) and most artists find the way that works for them.

Both block printing (using relief) and screen printing (using a stencil) can create great designs for fabric or surfaces.

The exact origin and date of this printing tool is unknown. Notice how it is made of metal; stamps can be made from many things, not just wood or rubber. See how intricate the designs are?

# Block Printing

Block printing is a carved stamping system in which a surface is carved to create "white" (sometimes negative) space. The carved surface, whether wood, stone, linoleum, or rubber, is essentially a stamp that can be used to produce the same image over and over again onto ceramics, animal skins, paper, or textiles. It is a simple process with three basic steps:

1. Carve the negative space out of the block.
2. Apply ink onto the raised surface of the block.
3. Press the block onto the fabric or other surface.

Block printing for decorative purposes dates far back in history, but as with many artistic media, it is difficult to determine exact origins. Asian, North African, and East Indian societies were some of the first to use block printing methods regularly to create beautiful, repeating textiles. The print textile industry became important in Europe around the twelfth century as the luxury market for textiles increased with the introduction of intricate woven and embroidered fabrics for society's upper crust. No matter the exact origins, block printing has a rich history within many cultures. It can be a simple way of bringing your designs to life on fabric.

## TOOLS AND EQUIPMENT

Block printing in your studio can be an amazing way to create repeat patterns and your own prints. It doesn't require a lot of space or expensive materials and can be incredibly freeing. Here are some things you should keep on hand:

**Carving Blocks** Several materials make suitable carving blocks, including blocks of wood, linoleum, and rubber. As long as you can carve it, you can use it. Wood is the most difficult to carve, requiring sharp tools because some basic woods splinter. But the effects can be very interesting and great to experiment with! Linoleum (stiff, but lasts a long time) or rubber stamp blocks, which are softer, are best for beginners. Keep a variety in different sizes in your studio or just get them as needed per project.

**Carving Tools** There are different types of carving tools with different weights, points, and tips to create varying effects and fine details. You can purchase carving tools from many places, and they range in quality. You can either draw your design directly on to the carving surface before you start to carve or carve freehand. Remember that carving tools are usually very sharp.

**Printing Fabrics** Choose your printing fabric carefully. To start, use sturdy woven cotton, linen, or silk. Knits are more difficult to print on because registration (page 106) on a stretchy fabric is not easy!

**Inks** Stock an assortment of fabric inks for printing on fabric and paper inks for printing on paper in the primary colors, plus black and white. You can use oil-based or water-based ink, but water-based ink is far easier to clean up. You can also save most water-based inks for a very long time in plastic storage containers.

**Glass Plate, Brayers, and Burnishing Tool** A glass plate without nicks or scratches is the ideal surface for rolling out the ink. A brayer, available in many sizes, is used to roll out the ink on the plate and on the carved block. A burnishing tool is used to rub the back of your paper or fabric to help press the ink consistently over the textile surface.

## LAYERS AND REGISTRATION

If you are working with one color, registration is simple because you don't have to worry about aligning multiple layers. You simply apply paint on the block and then apply the block onto the fabric.

When you are working with multiple color layers, each color needs its own block, and each block needs some type of clear registration marking to align the blocks on top of each other to create the design as intended. Apply the different color blocks, starting with the lightest color and moving to the darkest. Though there are many ways of registering images, including fancy tools, you can simply mark the corner where the block should align with a pencil, fabric marker, or tape. If you are using the same exact size block for each layer, you can use the same mark to align each block so that the images are aligned.

If you don't want to make a separate block for each color, you can create what is called a reductive print. Begin by carving the lightest color layer and use it to print as many copies as desired (a full edition) or as much yardage as desired. Then carve your next color layer in the same block. In effect, you are reducing the same block to your final layer. With this method, you cannot go back to print more because each layer is destroyed as you carve the next successive layer.

## CARVING YOUR BLOCK

Block printing, or any kind of relief printing, can be used to print negative or positive images. A positive image means that you are carving away the negative space to print the image. Negative printing means that you are carving out the image you want to create in white by leaving the negative image to print. It is very important in block and relief printing that you carve your image in reverse.

## INKING YOUR BLOCK AND PRINTING

Apply ink with the brayer onto a glass plate or directly on the carved surface. If the ink is on the plate, press the carved block into the ink to transfer it onto the block.

You can print by either placing the block face down onto the printing fabric (or other surface) or place the printing fabric on top of the block. If you are placing the block face down on the surface, apply even pressure from above the block. If you are placing the block face up, with the fabric or paper over it with the right side down, use a burnishing tool to rub the entire surface in a circular motion to ensure the transfer of the ink.

> **TIP** | **Watch Your Fingers**
>
> Be very careful to keep your hands out of the tool's path. A good way to do this is to hold your arms and hands with your elbows outwards. Always keep the hand holding the carving block behind the tool, never in front in case you slip forward. You can also use a carving board, which helps keep your carving surface in place so your arms don't have to!

# PROJECT:
# Block-Printed Pillow Cover

Depending on your level of interest in block print-ing, you can keep it very simple or increase your precision and skill to get highly intricate designs using fine tools. The very textured affect can be a nice addition.

## TOOLS FOR PRINTING

- Pencil
- Paper
- Blank rubber block for carving
- Brayer, at least as wide at the printing image
- Glass plate
- Carving tools of various sizes and shapes

## MATERIALS FOR PRINTING

- 1 yard (0.9 m) of 45" (114.3 cm)-wide plain or colored cotton or muslin fabric
- Water-based fabric ink

## TOOLS FOR SEWING

- Sewing machine
- Scissors
- Iron and ironing board
- Measuring tape

## MATERIALS FOR SEWING

- Thread
- 6" (15.2 cm) strip of 1" (2.5 cm)-wide Velcro

**ABOVE** Here is a finished pillow us-ing the artwork of Alexandra Labriola. It is hand printed and sewn! This is an easy way to update your home décor or make simple home goods for sale or gifts.

**BELOW** Block printing does not require too many materials and can create endless fun with a design that can be used over and over. All these items are easy to find.

# PRINTING INSTRUCTIONS

1. Draw out a simple design on paper. For this project, draw a one-color block that can be repeated.

2. Transfer your drawing onto your rubber block using transfer paper or draw it directly on the block. Remember, your image will be printed in reverse. You can use the light from a window or light box to create a mirror image. **[A]**

3. Use the carving tools to create the image. **[B]** Anything you carve away will be negative space. **[C]** Anything raised will accept ink and will be stamped onto the fabric. Experiment with a spare piece of rubber before carving the block. **[D]**

4. Mix the desired ink color, following the package instructions. We suggest testing the color on a fabric swatch first to be sure it is what you want.

5. Dab a small amount of ink on the top of the glass plate and use the brayer to roll the ink evenly out onto the glass. **[E]** Change the direction of the rolling motion many times, so that you have an even distribution. The brayer and ink will make a nice crackling sound when the adhesiveness is correct. **[F]**

6. With the charged brayer, roll the ink across the face of the carved block. **[G]** Roll and make sure the carving is correct and that you have ink in all the desired locations on the block.

7. Press your fabric flat and pin it to a padded surface. If you want to print as a repeat, mark the desired stamp locations with an invisible ink pen.

8. Place the inked stamp face down onto the first marked location. **[H]** Apply pressure evenly. Remove the stamp from the fabric and repeat as many times as desired. Let dry. **[I, J]**

9. After the fabric has dried, heat set it by putting it in the dryer for several minutes.

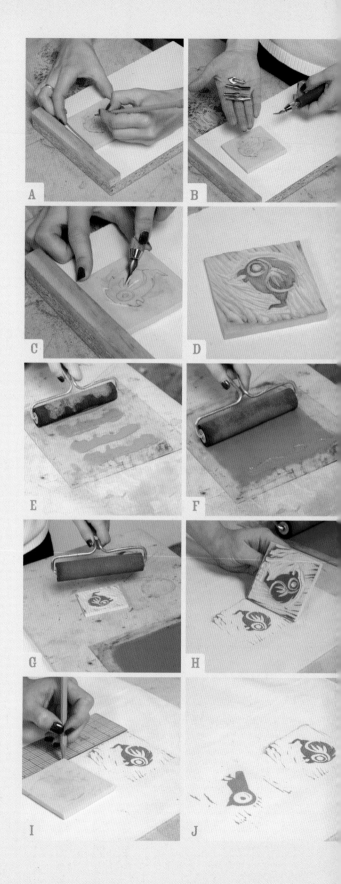

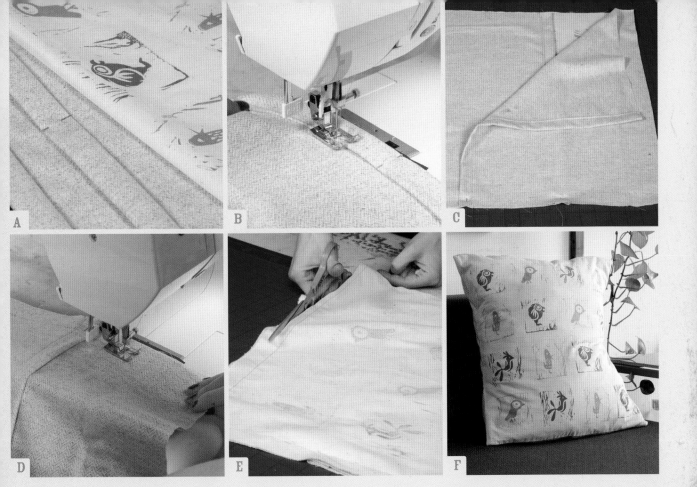

## Sewing Instructions

These instructions are for a 12 inch x 12 inch (30.5 x 30.5 cm) pillowcase. You can make it any size as long as you keep in mind the size and shape of the block printed design and how much yardage you created.

**10.** Cut out one 13 inch x 13 inch (33 x 33 cm) square and two pieces, each 13 inches x 8 inches (33 x 20.3 cm). This allows for ½ inch (1.3 cm) seam allowances.

**11.** The two smaller pieces will be the back of the pillow with a flap closure. Fold one shorter edge of each piece ½ inch (1.3 cm) to the wrong side and then ½ inch (1.3 cm) again. Press to hem the edges and straight stitch close to the inside folded edge. **[A, B]**

**12.** Lay the block printed fabric face up. Line up the two back pieces so that they overlap to be the same size as the front piece, face down. **[C]**

**13.** Pin the two squares together with the right sides facing each other. Sew around the edges of the square with ½ inch (1.3 cm) seam allowances, pivot at the corners. Trim any threads and the seam allowance, especially at the corners. **[D, E]**

**14.** Turn your pillowcase right side out through the flap opening. Insert a standard pillow form for a pillow cover completely designed by you! **[F]**

# Screen Printing

Screen printing is the process of pushing ink through a woven mesh screen onto the desired surface. The image is created by resist, or blocking parts of the screen so the ink can't pass through, usually by using a stencil. Simple stencils can be cut from paper. More intricate stencils are burned onto a screen using a light sensitive emulsion. This section focuses on the use of photo-emulsion to create a stencil that will last for a very long time.

The popular media of screen printing first appeared as we would recognize it in China sometime between 960-1279 CE and soon after in Japan and other Asian countries. Though block printing had been done for many centuries before, the method of using woven silk mesh to reproduce images on textiles was quite advanced. It became popular in the western world around the late eighteenth century, when silk mesh was more readily available from the East. Although the exact person responsible for inventing screen printing is unknown, it was first patented in England by Samuel Simon in 1907. Its popularity for printing wallpaper and fabric yardage grew rapidly, forcing many printing houses to keep trade secrets. Screen printing allowed for sharper-edged images, and eventually led to the giant industry that printing is today. Screen printing as an art form and avenue of creative expression entered the world of fine art in the 1960s thanks to people like Andy Warhol, Robert Rauschenberg, and Harry Gottlieb.

## TOOLS AND EQUIPMENT

The tools and equipment for screen printing are few if you keep it simple. However, once you are hooked on screen printing and plan to do it often, it may be worth investing in professional tools and equipment. The complexity really depends on the type of stencil you plan to use. If you want to use photo emulsion to burn an image onto a screen, you'll need equipment, whereas hand-cutting paper stencils is quite straightforward. The basic requirements are as follows:

**Stencils** No matter how you make your stencil, it is fundamental to screen printing. You can draw and cut a stencil from waxed paper, or you can use photoactive emulsion to burn the stencil image on a screen (see page 117). Paper stencils last for several printing passes, but if you want a stencil that can be used repeatedly for a long time, you'll need to use photoreactive emulsion and burn a screen. The emulsions are liquids that can be hand painted onto the screen, which harden to create the resist. In the early twentieth century, Roy Beck, Edward Owens, and Charles Peter developed the first chemical photoreactive emulsion. Over time, the recipe has become safer and more suitable for use in home studios, schools, and smaller print shops.

If you are creating stencils via a photo emulsion process, you'll need a safety light that does not effect the light-sensitive chemicals. Usually they have a red or yellow glow.

**Screens** You can purchase mesh screens in a variety of sizes and mesh counts (the number of threads per inch) specifically for screen printing. For fine detailed images, you'll want a higher mesh count, whereas for less detailed images, a lower count will suffice. They are made with aluminum or wood frames. Wood frames are generally cheaper, but do not last as long as aluminum frames because they warp over time. However, if the mesh rips on an aluminum screen, you need to have it professionally restretched, whereas with wood frames you can replace the mesh with a staple gun.

**Inks and Dyes** While printing with ink is very popular and commonly used for printing t-shirts and tote bags, when it comes to textile and surface design, there is a big difference between printing with inks and printing with dyes. Inks rest on the surface of the fabric, while dyes absorb into the individual fibers of the fabric, integrating with the actual structure. Since the dye actually becomes part of the fabric, the fabric remains soft. Ink, on the other hand, rests on the fabric surface so the fabric has a stiffness to it.

Fabric and paper inks are packaged ready to print. They will last for a long time as long as they're stored in plastic storage containers. Dyes, whether natural or synthetic, require mixing pigment with paste, usually an alginate, to create a substance that combines with the color and can be pushed through the screen like ink. Dyes usually last no more than 24 to 48 hours and must be stored in the refrigerator.

This screen hinge system works great for screen printing one-off items such as T-shirts or bags. You can purchase the hinge sets at a printing supply store or online and attach them to plywood to make a movable station. This makes registration simple because you can mark the printing location right onto the board.

**Squeegees, Spatulas, and Plastic Knives** You'll need rubber squeegees in several sizes for working with different size images. A squeegee pushes the ink through the mesh onto your surface. Spatulas and plastic knives are useful for mixing inks, applying inks onto the screen for printing, and cleaning up.

If you intend to use the photo emulsion technique, you'll also need the following equipment.

- Light table with florescent lights that allow light sensitive chemicals to accept an image

- Photo emulsion to coat your screen—There are many types, so please ask for help at the store based on your needs

- Scoop Coater to evenly coat a screen

- Dark room or dark area is essential

---

**TIP** **Holding Your Screen in Place**

For creating one-off screen prints at home, you can make a simple board like the one shown here. With just a piece of plywood and a screen printing hinge system, you'll have a portable station that holds your screen in place. Mark the location of the printable surface so the image is printed in the same place with each pass.

# HOW TO:
# Create a Repeat Design

There are simpler ways to create a repeat design on the computer; however, understanding this basic technique and theory is important for your general knowledge and ability to create successful repeat prints. Remember, this is not necessary to learn, but it is important to comprehend how you can create a stencil to print in various colors.

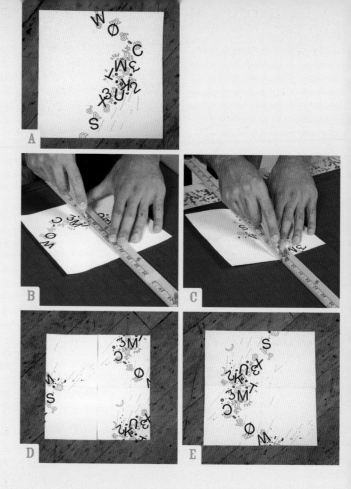

## TOOLS:

- 8" x 8" (20.3 x 20.3 cm) white paper, scissors, and assortment of drawing utensils

## INSTRUCTIONS:

1. Draw a simple design so part of it goes off the paper. Don't start with anything too elaborate. **[A]**

2. Cut your paper in half vertically to create two 8 x 4 (20.3 x 10.2 cm) pieces. Take the left half and move it to the right side of the right half. **[B]**

3. Look at your image now. What do you see happening? What do you need to draw to complete the image you started? What holes do you see, and how would you use the new negative space? Continue drawing.

4. Now cut these in half, horizontally, to create four 4 x 4 (10.2 x 10.2 cm) pieces. Move the two bottom pieces to the top of the other two pieces. Again, what do you see? What needs to be done to complete the image? What does the negative space look like? **[C]**

5. Now move the two right-hand quarters to the left side of the left quarters. Observe how your image has changed. Continue drawing, as needed. **[D]**

6. Move the top two quarters back down to the bottom. You are back at the starting point. What does the paper look like now? **[E]** You have now created a print design for repeat screen printing that should be (hopefully!) seamless (meaning you can't tell where it begins and ends).

7. You can use this image to create a stencil, with either the cut stencil method (opposite) or by burning the layers onto screens using photo emulsion (page 117). Each color you use will need to be its own layer. Keep your first attempt at a repeat design very simple so that your registration is not too difficult (page 106).

8. This specific "how to" is about creating a design image, not a stencil. You can use this repeat image however you like; you can even send it away to be digitally printed!

# HOW TO:

# Make a Hand-Cut Stencil

Using hand-cut stencils is fast and simple and will keep the screen printing process low maintenance. We encourage you to explore this in greater depth than what we have here. One of our favorite resources is *Printing by Hand* by Lena Corwin. In this book, Corwin covers all the ways you can print by hand at home using very simple techniques that don't require special equipment.

## TOOLS

- Stretched screen (for screen printing), contact paper, X-acto knife, self-healing cutting mat

## INSTRUCTIONS:

1. On the paper side of your contact paper (not the peel-off side), draw your design with a pencil. Keep in mind that floating parts, such as the center of the lowercase *e*, are lost at times. With contact paper, though, you can stick that part back on the screen.

2. Place your cutting mat down with contact paper over it. Cut out the stencil with the X-acto knife.

3. Peel off the back of the contact paper and adhere it to the front of the screen. This stencil will remain intact for a good number of passes before the paper falls apart or starts to peel off. It's so easy! See page 106 for applying ink or dye and printing tips.

# PROJECT:

# How to Make a Light Box

If you are excited to begin screen printing and plan to use the photo emulsion method (see chapter 6), you can make a light box to expose your screens. It is also handy for tracing imagery onto fabric for embroidery. A homemade light box can be as small as you would like for storage purposes, and it's easy on the wallet.

This light box measures 30" x 24" (76.2 x 61 cm), large enough to accommodate many screen sizes but small enough to store easily.

## MATERIALS

- 1 piece of ply wood cut to 30" x 24" 76.2 cm x 61 cm)
- 2 pieces of 1 x 8" plywood, cut to 30" (76.2 cm) long
- 2 pieces of 1 x 8" plywood, cut to 22" (55.9 cm) long
- 1 piece of 30" x 24" (76.2 x 61 cm) glass, with no UV filter
- Fluorescent lighting fixtures with exposed, not covered bulbs (we used two 24" [61 cm] long units, with two light bulbs) Note: *If you are inexperienced with wiring, seek help from someone more knowledgable.*
- 4 Fluorescent light bulbs, with no UV filter (appropriate wattage for purchased fixtures)
- Small container of white paint (enough to paint the inside of the box)
- Thick, small furniture pads (for the bottom of the finished unit)

## TOOLS

- Paintbrush
- Drill to fit 2" (5.1 cm) flat head screws
- 2" (5.1 cm) flat head screws
- Several bolts, nuts, 1" (2.5 cm) washers, grip washers
- Wrench
- Surge protector
- On/off switch
- 2" (5.1 cm) white gaffers tape
- Strong, double-sided adhesive tape
- Pencil
- Wood glue, optional
- Wood putty, optional

## INSTRUCTIONS

1.  Cut the wood to the listed dimensions.

2.  Construct the outer part of the box into a 30 x 24- inch (76.2 x 61 cm) rectangle. Fasten the 1 x 8-inch wood pieces together using the drill and 2-inch (5.1 cm) screws. The shorter 22-inch (55.9 cm) pieces fit between (inside) the 30-inch (76.2 cm) pieces. Use two screws per side, positioned at least 1 inch (2.5 cm) from the edge with approximately 5 inch (12.7 cm) or 6 inch (15.2 cm) between the screws. You may want to dab a small amount of wood glue on the ends of the wood pieces first, but this is optional. Another aesthetic decision may be to fill the screw holes with wood putty and paint the entire outside of the box if seeing the screws bothers you. You can paint the outside of the box later. **[A]**

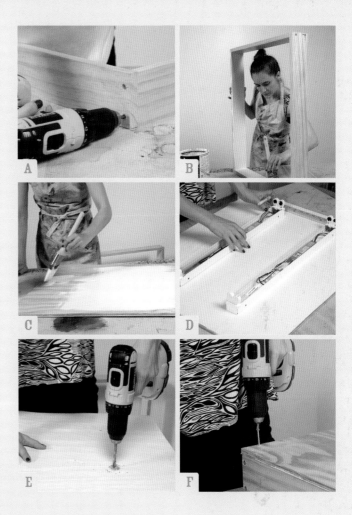

3.  Paint a thick coat of white paint on the inside of the rectangular frame. The white paint on the inside of the box creates a reflective surface and helps to evenly distribute light. Paint one side of the 30-inch x 24-inch (76.2 x 61 cm) plywood. Set the painted wood aside to dry. **[B, C]**

4.  Place the florescent light fixtures (without the bulbs in) in the center of the dry 30-inch x 24-inch (76.2 x 61 cm) piece of plywood. Measure to ensure that they are centered both vertically and horizontally and pencil-mark the board for placement. Pencil the screw holes in the bottom of the fixtures on the board also. **[D]**

5.  Choose a bolt and drill bit that fit through the holes in the fixtures and drill holes through the wood in all the marked screw holes. **[E]**

6.  Place the rectangular frame on the floor and the 30-inch x 24-inch (76.2 x 61 cm) piece (white paint facing down) over it. Drill the board to the frame with 2-inch (5.1 cm) screws, starting at the corners and then between the corners, on all sides. **[F]**

**7.** Flip the constructed box over. Lifting the box slightly off the floor, insert four bolts through the drilled holes from the back so they extend inside the box. **[G]**

**8.** Slide the light fixtures onto the bolts through the holes in the fixtures. Put one larger washer, then one grip washer onto each bolt. Secure the washers in place with a nut and tightly screw the nuts in place. You are now ready to wire your lights. **[H, I]**

**9.** Ask someone with significant experience in electrical wiring to wire the lights so they plug into the wall, using the surge protector, and to install the on/off switch on the outside of the box.

**10.** Insert the bulbs and test that the fixtures work. If so, great! You can complete the light box. **[J]**

**11.** Position a piece of double-sided adhesive tape on the top edge of each side of the frame. Remove the backing. Carefully place the glass down on top of the frame. **[K]**

**12.** Wrap the 2 inch (5.1 cm) gaffers tape around each edge of the frame, securing the glass. This will also ensure that the edges are not sharp. **[L, M]**

**13.** You can place your felt furniture pads on the bottom of the unit now, before putting on the glass, which will make it heavy. **[N]**

Congratulations! You have made your own light box. Be sure to store it flat when it isn't being used.

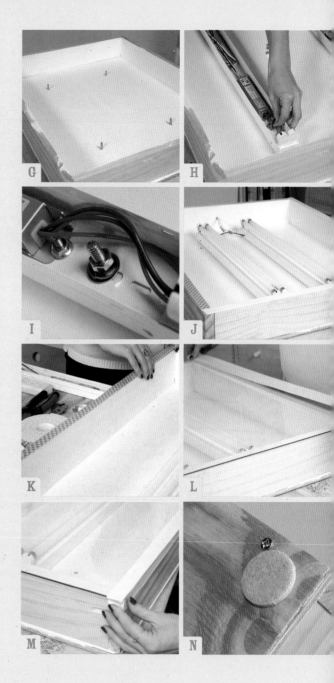

# Tutorial: Burning and Coating a Screen

This method of screen printing requires a darkroom and some professional equipment and is the most widely used screen printing method today, mostly due to the durability of the stencil. It is also popular because design lines can be very exact and you can use photographic images.

## TOOLS:

- Framed screen (for screen printing)
- Scoop coater
- Photo emulsion*
- Darkroom w/ safety light
- Fan, optional

*There are many types of emulsion, with varying shelf-life. Some are premixed, and others require mixing a sensitizer into the liquid.

## COATING THE SCREEN

Coat both sides of a screen with a light sensitive emulsion that will later be exposed to light.

## INSTRUCTIONS:

1. Select a silk screen that is the appropriate size and mesh count for the image you are printing. The mesh count refers to the number of threads per inch on the woven fabric. Generally, you will use a higher mesh count for more detailed images. Keep your printing area in mind, as well as the overall frame dimension (the frame in total). Generally, there is a 2½-inch (6.4 cm) border on every side of the screen from the edge of the wood or aluminum frame.

2. Pour a small amount of photo emulsion along the inside of the scoop coater. The scoop coater should fit easily inside the frame with at least a 1-inch (2.5 cm) border. Make sure the emulsion is evenly distributed inside the scoop.

3. With the screen upright and stable, place the scoop at a 45-degree angle to the screen, starting at the bottom allowing the thick emulsion to meet the screen. Tilt side to side to distribute the liquid. Apply pressure, drag the scoop upwards at the 45- degree angle, evenly coating the screen. You may need to do multiple runs to try to eliminate any layer lines you create in multiple passes. Repeat for the opposite side.

*(continued)*

4. When you have an even coat on your screen, place it in the dark room to dry completely. Use a fan to speed up the drying process.

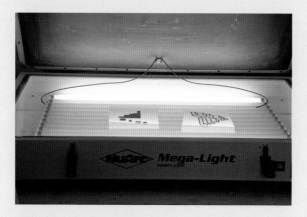

## BURNING THE SCREEN

Burning the screen is the process of imprinting the image onto the screen to create a stencil. The ultra-violet rays involved, whether you use a vacuum table or a handmade light box (see page 114), expose the light-sensitive emulsion to any part of the screen that isn't covered by the stencil. The image is then washed out of the screen, leaving the stencil behind.

## TOOLS:

- Coated screen (see page 117)
- Stencil, design in black pen or paint on acetate or transparent paper (see step 1, page 117)
- Transparent tape
- Vacuum exposure unit or UV light table
- Water hose

## INSTRUCTIONS:

5. Prep your image. Photo emulsion creates a stencil on the screen by using a black image to block the area that you would like to print. Any area that is blocked will not allow the emulsion to activate, so the unblocked emulsion will wash away after burning. To create your stencil, you can draw with permanent marker on acetate or print with black ink directly from a printer onto acetate paper.

6. Tape your image, marked on the transparent or acetate paper, to the front (flat side) of the screen with transparent tape.

7. Place the screen face (stencil side down) on the center of the exposure unit **[A]**. On a vacuum table, which uses suction pressure to keep the screen in place, there are two vacuum tubes extending from the unit. Place both of these tubes on the inside of the screen, close to the sides of the frame **[B]**. Close the top and lock it in place **[C]**.

---

**TIP** **Using a Homemade Light Box**

If you are using a homemade light box like the one constructed earlier in this chapter (page 114), you'll need a few things to mimic the action of the vacuum table. During the burning, you will need to cover your screen with thick, black felt, draped over the screen and light box. You will also need something heavy to keep pressure on the screen; heavy books will do the trick. Purchase a good loud timer as well, because the light box won't turn off automatically like a professional unit. You'll have to flip that switch yourself! Burning takes between 15 and 30 minutes in the professional unit and up to two hours in the handmade version.

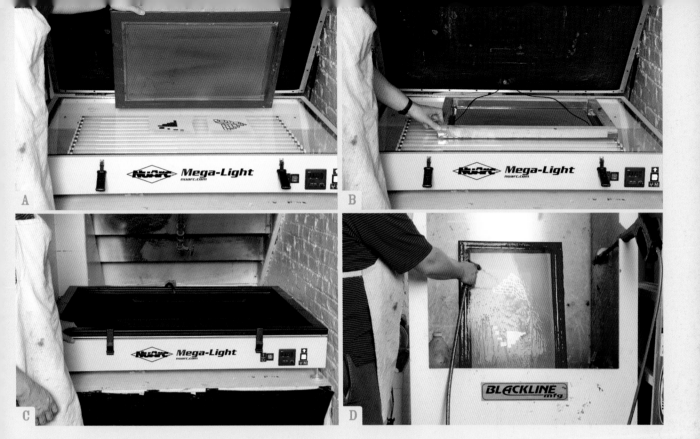

A

B

C

D *BLACKLINE* mfg

8. Depending on the type of unit you have, buttons and placement will vary. However, there are two things that always need to happen: the vacuum needs to be turned on and the air completely sucked out, and next the UV lights need to be turned on for a certain amount of time to expose the screen. Length of exposure will vary, so you may have to experiment.

9. When the time has elapsed and the light has turned off, unlock the top of the unit. Take the screen off the bed. The image you exposed will start to develop over the next minute and show up on the screen. When you see the image developing, remove the acetate.

10. Using a normal-pressure hose, spray the screen in the washing area or washout booth. The emulsion in the area of the image will start to come off, leaving the image area clear for ink to pass through. Hold the screen up to the light to make

sure that all the emulsion has completely washed out. Also, check to see if there are holes in the emulsion coating. If the emulsion is not solid in the surrounding area, cover the holes with packing tape so that ink can't pass through **[D]**.

11. You are ready for printing (see page 120).

You are ready for printing (see page 120).

| TIP | **Transparency in a Pinch**

Regarding your image, you can always print an opaque black image on acetate since you need it to be transparent. However, in a pinch, you can also draw or print directly on computer paper and soak the paper in oil to make it transparent. Cleanup is not fun, but it works!

# PROJECT:
# Simple Screen-Printed Tote

Screen printing can be done on so many surfaces and decorate countless things. We have created a simple tote bag with a two-layer print. Check out other methods of design on the exact same type of bag in the Dyeing chapter. Just imagine what happens when you combine these two methods!

## TOOLS

- 2" (5.1 cm)-wide spatula or plastic spackle knife
- Squeegee in the appropriate size
- Masking tape
- Piece of cardboard
- Drop cloth or tarp

## MATERIALS

- Exposed screen (see page 118) of any desired image
- Fabric ink in two desired colors
- Plain cotton tote bag

## INSTRUCTIONS

1. Prep your printing area by laying a drop cloth or tarp on a padded surface or a clean, hard surface. This project is a good example of a time that the one-off hinge system would work well (see Tip on page 111).

2. Place the cardboard on the inside of the tote bag, underneath the area you will be printing to prevent bleeding through to the other side.

3. The print shown here uses two layers, one for the body of the "blocks" and one for the outline. Burn both stencils (page 118); we were able to fit both on the same screen since the images both fit comfortably on the screen.

4. Place the first stencil layer, the blocks, on the front of the tote bag and line up the tote and screen so the image prints at the desired location. With the screen flat against the tote bag, use the knife/spatula to evenly distribute a line of red ink across the area where you will be passing the squeegee **[A]**.

5. Place your squeegee in the line of ink so that the bottom edge is evenly coated **[B]**. Be sure to use a squeegee length that is appropriate for the image; it should not be smaller than the width of your image or much larger, either.

**120**    THE TEXTILE ARTIST'S STUDIO HANDBOOK

6. When the ink is evenly distributed on the squeegee, make your first pass over the image; this
is called flooding the screen **[C]**. The ink will be
pushed through the screen and moved to the opposite side of the image **[D]**.

7. Lift the squeegee and make an additional pass
over the image, pulling the majority of the ink with
it. Hold the squeegee at a 45 degree angle to the
screen with one or two hands (depending on the
size of the image) and pull the squeegee toward
you, applying even steady pressure and maintaining the angle.

8. Remove the excess ink from the screen and
squeegee with the plastic knife and put it back in
the ink container.

9. Lift the screen, separating it from the tote bag.
*Voila!* You have completed the first layer **[E]**.

10. For the second layer, or black outline shown here,
wait at least 30 minutes for the ink to dry. While
you're waiting, clean the screen with a normal
pressure hose, removing all signs of the first color
ink. Your screen must be dry before starting the
second layer.

11. Repeat the same steps to print the second layer;
however, before you flood the screen, make sure
the layers are registered as desired and the second layer is where it belongs **[F, G, H, I, J, K]**.

12. After you print the second layer, you can easily
heat-set the tote bag using a cotton rag and hot
iron. When the ink is dry, place a cotton rag over
the image. Heat an iron to the cotton setting and
iron over the cotton rag for a minute or two. This
will heat-set the ink, helping it adhere to the fabric
so that the image does not wash off.

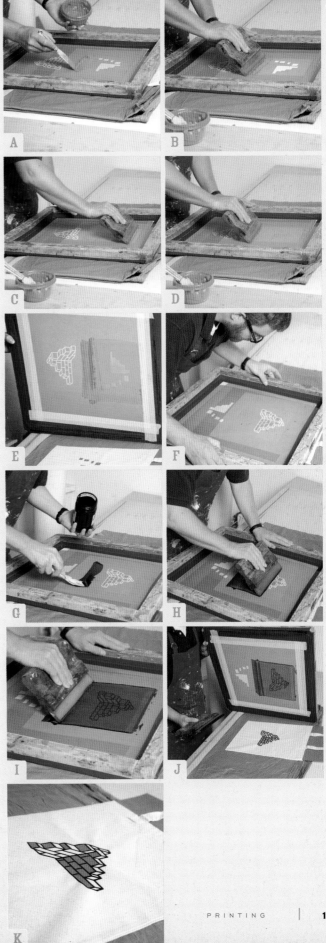

CHAPTER

**7**

# Dyeing

**ABOVE** Shown here are some common naturally dyed yarns held in glass jars for display as part of a piece entitled "Cures for Depressions" by Tali Weinberg shown at the Textile Arts Center in July 2011.

**RIGHT** Natural dyeing uses many of the same tools and equipment as dyeing with synthetic pigments, but the dyes and chemicals are very different.

**Dyeing is the process of applying a colored substance (dye) to a substrate (fiber, yarn, fabric, etc).** The dye, which is almost always soluble in water (or can become soluble in water), penetrates the structure of the fibers to form chemical bonds, changing their color. It is the choosing and working with the actual dyes that makes this process so exciting. You can find dyestuff all around you, from animals, vegetables, plants, and chemicals, and you can experiment to create beautiful colors. The possibilities are endless, and the process is simple and enriching.

There is sometimes confusion about the differences between dye and pigment, the substances able to provide color. Pigments are not generally soluble in water and to be applied as a coloring material, they need to be mixed with a liquid that acts as a dispersing agent or vehicle. Once the liquid dries, it holds the pigment to the surface of the fiber. In most cases, dyes are used to add color to textiles, paper, and other substances, while pigments are used for coloring paints, inks, cosmetics, and plastics.

## The History of Dyeing

For thousands of years, people have been dyeing yarns, fabrics, and clothes using materials from the world around them, including roots, flowers, fruits, insects, and minerals. The earliest written record of the use of natural dyes comes from China, dated around 2600 BCE.

It was the desire for brighter and different colors that lead to the development of simple and complex dyeing procedures, which were passed on from generation to generation. Some natural dyes were very hard to obtain and/or use, so the colors they produced inevitably became the most valued. For instance, before the invention of synthetic dyes, purple was mainly obtained from a gland in the sea snail. It is not difficult to imagine why purple became the color associated with royalty and power in so many cultures. Just consider the number of snails needed to produce even the smallest amount of dye!

Natural dyes, although ubiquitous, had limitations. Not all the natural dyes were light resistant, meaning they faded over time. Some fibers, such as cotton, were difficult to dye into bright colors. Before the sixteenth century, when trade routes were limited, only local materials could be used as dye sources. However, since the first synthetic dye was only invented in 1856, it's impossible not to be amazed by the mastership of skill achieved with natural dyes prior to the nineteenth century.

The eventual invention and popularization of synthetic dyes provided easy and cheap access to bright and varied colors. Slowly, natural dyeing techniques became less popular, even in less industrialized countries. However, the revival of natural dyes that started in the 1970s continues, especially as the world becomes more aware of the limitations of synthetic dyes and the consequences of their use to the environment. Significant numbers of fashion designers and artists are reverting to the use of natural dyes as a more eco-friendly material choice and as a way to reconnect with nature and traditional practices. Thankfully, history, current experimentation, and the joy of working in textile media provide good resources for working with natural dyes. If you enjoy gathering materials, hikes in the woods, and a bit of chemistry, you'll love dying your own yarns and fabrics.

# Types of Dyes

Dyes are either natural or synthetic and can be further divided according to their chemistry.

## SYNTHETIC DYES

These dyes are made of organic compounds and were developed to improve the quality of natural dyes. They are easy to handle and colorfast, providing solutions to the main complaint of natural dyes.

**Acid Dyes**  Acid dyes react best with the protein fibers under slightly acidic conditions and hot temperatures. They can be purchased in the supermarket.

**Fiber Reactive Dyes**  Fiber Reactive dyes have the ability to react directly with the fiber, forming a permanent bond. The dye molecule actually becomes one with the fiber, resulting in permanent color. They were developed in the UK in the 1950s as an alternative for dyeing cellulose fibers. They offer several advantages: They can be mixed at low temperatures, they're relatively nontoxic, they're inexpensive, they provide a great variety of bright colors, and they don't lose their color through exposure to light or washing. These are the best dyes to use on cotton. The most popular fiber reactive dye is Procion MX, which is suitable for beginners and practiced dyers alike. You'll also find them with generic brand names, sold by several dye suppliers. The project on page 136, Space-Dyed Yarn, is done with fiber reactive dyes.

**ABOVE**  Shown here is linen fabric dyed with Procion dyes using a tie-dye folding technique.

### TIP | Measure the pH

pH is a measure of the acidity or alkalinity of an aqueous solution. The pH scale runs from 1–14, with 7 being neutral, 1 being most acidic, and 14 being most alkaline. Pure water has a pH neutral, lemon juice and vinegar have acidic pHs, and soda ash, slacked lime, and lye have alkaline pHs. You can measure the pH of a liquid with pH testing strips that change color when they come in contact with a certain pH. It is important to check the pH of your tap water and your dyeing solutions because it can affect the outcome of the colors, especially when working with natural dyes.

**Recommended Method of Synthetic Dyeing According to Fiber Content**

| | FIBERS | | | | | | | |
|---|---|---|---|---|---|---|---|---|
| **DYES** | Cotton | Linen, Hemp | Silk | Wool | Rayon | Polyester | Nylon | Acrylic |
| Fiber Reactive | X | X | X | No | X | No | No | No |
| Acid | No | No | X | X | No | No | No | No |
| Disperse | No | No | No | No | No | X | X | No |

**Disperse Dyes** These dyes were developed to dye polyester and require hot temperatures. This is not an easy process for artists new to the media.

## Natural Dyes

Dyes can be found in your own natural environment. Natural dyes have undeniable aesthetic appeal, but they can be more difficult to work with than synthetic dyes, although wool fibers are particularly suited to natural dyes. Cotton is less suitable and synthetic fibers usually don't accept natural dyes. There are three common forms of natural dyes.

**Mordant Dyes** Most natural dyes, including madder, weld, and cochineal, fall into this category. These dyes require the presence of a mordant, a substance that helps "fix" the dyes to the fibers because it has an affinity to both. Mordants are often metal salts (such as alum, iron, copper, and tin salts) but can also be tannins (existent in tea) or certain acids, such as oxalic acid, which exists in rhubarb leaves. The mordant can be applied before, during, or after the dyeing process, but it is usually done before dyeing (see page 131). Sometimes, mordants are applied after dyeing to vary the hues. For example, after-dyeing yellow fibers in an iron solution will change most to green and dull most other colors.

The most commonly used mordant is alum (aluminum sulfate), and it is good for wool and silk fibers. Cellulose fibers can be harder to dye and normally require a stronger mordant, such as aluminum acetate or a combination of alum and tannins.

Both alum and aluminum acetate have the great advantage of retaining the colors of the natural dyes.

**Direct, or Substantive Dyes** Direct (or substantive) dyes are applied to textiles without a mordant or any other processing. They are the dyes most often used at home for simple dye jobs and include turmeric, achiote seeds, and walnut hulls.

**Vat Dyes** Vat dyes don't require a mordant. They must be in the water-soluble form to penetrate the fibers and then be converted to the nonsoluble form to get trapped in the fiber structure. This requires an oxidation-reduction reaction, which can be difficult without professional equipment. Examples include indigo and Tyrian Purple.

**Recommended Method of Natural Dyeing According to Fiber Content**

| DYES | FIBERS | | | | | | | |
|---|---|---|---|---|---|---|---|---|
| | Cotton | Linen, Hemp | Silk | Wool | Rayon | Polyester | Nylon | Acrylic |
| Direct | X | X | X | X | No | No | No | No |
| Mordant | X | X | X | X | No | No | No | No |
| Vat | X | X | X | X | No | No | No | No |

## Well-Known Historic Natural Dyes

| DYE NAME | PLANT/ANIMAL | PART USED | COLOR |
|----------|--------------|-----------|-------|
| Madder | *Rubia tinctoria* | roots | orange–red–purple |
| Cochineal | *Dactylopius coccus* | whole animal | orange–red–purple |
| Brazilwood | *Caesalpinia echinata* | hardwood | red–purple |
| Quebracho | *Schinopsis* spp | hardwood | red |
| Logwood | *Haematoxylum campechianum* | hardwood | purple–grey–black |
| Tyrian purple | Different species of sea snails | mucous secretion from snail's gland | purple |
| Indigo | *Indigofera tinctoria, Isatis tinctoria, Polygonum tinctorium* | leaves | blue |
| Weld | *Reseda luteola* | whole plant | yellow |
| Old fustic | *Maclura tinctoria* | whole plant | yellow |

## Common Natural Dyes

| DYE NAME | PART USED | COLOR |
|----------|-----------|-------|
| Marigold | flowers | yellow |
| Tickseed | flowers | yellow |
| Yellow onions | skins | yellow–orange |
| Avocados | peels, pits | pink–grey |
| Turmeric | root | yellow |
| Rhubarb | leaves | yellow |
| Blackberries | berries | purple–grey |
| Black Walnuts | hulls | yellow–brown |
| St. John's Wort | whole plant | yellow |
| Red cabbage | leaves | purple–grey |
| Pomegranate | rinds | tan |

# Equipment and Materials

The simplest dyeing methods don't require elaborate setups and expensive equipment.

## Equipment

Much of this equipment you probably already own, but reserve dyeing equipment for the dye lab.

**Pots and Kettles** You'll need a variety of different size pots and kettles for dye baths and for mordanting.

- For natural dyes, stainless steel won't alter the color.

- Take advantage of a cast iron pot if you are working with natural dyes; you won't have to add a mordant because the iron salts from the pot will do the job.

- Aluminum, enamel, and porcelain are suitable for most other dyes.

**Plastic and Glass Containers** You'll need an assortment of bottles and jars and plastic containers. You can reuse items such as pickle jars from your kitchen.

**Miscellaneous Supplies**

- Plastic or stainless steel measuring cups and spoons for measuring powders and liquids

- Scale for measuring powders and fabric/yarn —Digital scales are best, with units in the metric system and a minimum capacity of 0.1 g.

- Stirring rods, whisks, and tongs to mix and rotate

- Hot plates, butane burners, or a stove top for projects that require hot temperatures

- Calculator to adapt recipes to your specifications

- Thermometer to monitor the temperature

- Waterproof pen and tape to label projects and experiments—Tyvek is a writable, waterproof material

- Aprons, gloves, respirator masks, and goggles as protection from dyes, mordants, and spills.

## Materials

These basic materials are good to have on hand.

- Aluminum sulfate (alum) is the main mordant used for dyeing natural fibers with natural dyes. We recommend it for dyeing wool, cotton, silk, and even bast fibers. It has a low toxicity and doesn't add color.

- Aluminum acetate is a fine white powder that is mainly used to mordant cotton and other bast fibers. Because it is so fine, extra safety precautions such as using a dust mask should be taken.

- Baking soda is similar to washing soda but not as strong. It can be used as a pH modifier and as an activator for fiber reactive dyes.

- Iron sulfate can be used as the main mordant or added to a natural dye solution as a color modifier.

- Natural extract dyes are powders created by the evaporation of water from the natural dye extraction solution. They're more concentrated than raw materials, so you'll need less. They dissolve in water.

- Natural Raw Materials Dyes are made from any natural material that you're able to extract color from.

- Soda ash (sodium carbonate), or washing soda, is a white powder. When mixed into a solution, it will make it alkaline. It's used as a pH modifier and as an activator for fiber reactive dyes.

- Synthrapol is a pH neutral soap used to scour fibers.

- Urea is a white granular substance that is mainly used when dyeing with fiber reactive dyes. It delays the drying process, allowing more time for the reaction between the fiber and the dye.

- Vinegar makes certain solutions acidic. It can also be mixed with water to rinse silk and wool fibers to enhance their softness and sheen after dyeing.

# Growing a Dye Garden

Plants, flowers, and even roots are a great source of natural dyes, and you can grow many of them in your garden or even on your fire escape or windowsill. However, before you start sourcing out seeds and making big dyeing plans, there are a few things you should consider when setting up your own dye garden. Refer to the chart on page 128 for easy and common plants and flowers to plant in your dye garden.

One good rule is to choose native plants, including ones that you've seen growing in your area. This way you'll be sure to start with plants that are suitable for your environment and climate because the dye content in plants is significantly influenced by temperature, humidity, and solar exposure.

Another important thing to consider is the part of the plant from which the dye will be extracted and the sustainability of actually growing and using the plant. For instance, marigolds have their greater dye content in the flowers, and they will keep blooming throughout the season if you keep picking the flowers. Madder, on the other hand, has its red dye in the roots, so you'll have to pick the whole plant to extract the dye.

Shown here are a range of colors that can be achieved using various natural dyes and mordants.

In addition to the location of the dye, consider how much dye a species will yield. Using madder as an example again, the minimum age for harvesting the madder roots is three years; as the plant ages, the dye content in the roots increases. And from one madder plant, you'll probably harvest enough dye for only a couple of yards of fabric and a few skeins of yarn.

## STARTING FROM SEEDS

You won't find most of the traditional dye-source plants in a nursery, so if you want to grow them, you'll have to start from seed. A wide selection of the good dye-plant seeds are available online at natural dyes suppliers.

Most seeds should be planted a couple of months before your last anticipated frost, but we strongly recommend that you refer to the instructions that are normally included in the seed packet. Generally, you'll put two to three seeds in a small container filled with seed starting soil (a soil rich in nutrients). Place the container(s) in a box with a transparent lid in a sunny indoor location and water regularly. You can find special boxes for seed starting in most gardening stores.

After the last frost (unless your seeds have other special instructions), move your seedlings outdoors as long as they seem big and resilient enough to handle weather conditions.

> ## TIP | Size of the Seeds
>
> Cover small seeds with a tiny layer of soil or even just rest them on the surface of the soil; bigger seeds should be sown deeper. A good rule of thumb is to cover the seeds with only as much soil as the actual seed size.

## STARTING FROM PLANTS

Whether you buy plants or grow seedlings inside, the best time to plant outside is after the last frost. By this time the weather conditions should be mild.

When you plant your garden, give consideration to the space certain plants will occupy once they are fully grown. Ask advice at your nursery or research specific plants to better plan an arrangement for your garden. Usually a full-grown plant will occupy between 1 and 3 feet (0.3 and 0.9 m) of space, but this can vary. Don't position the plants too close to each other or they'll compete for sun, nutrients, and water. Also, if you're planting a species of plant known for expanding, you should probably put it in a container to prevent it from taking over the whole garden. Also consider the amount of sun that shines on your garden; most plants prefer full sun, but some might be more tolerant of shade, so plan accordingly.

Before you plant, prepare the soil with a mixture of pot soil and compost. Dig and mix the soil well and wet it. If any of the plants are big enough, open up the roots. Dig a hole for each plant a couple of inches deep, place the plant in it, adjust the soil around it, and water generously.

## MAINTENANCE AND PLANNING THE NEXT SEASON

Monitor and keep notes about the growth of your plants throughout the season; check their reaction to the climate, soil, water, etc. Some plants might need to be trimmed if they grow too much. At the end of the season, review your notes and make a garden log. Note which plants did well and which ones didn't. In some cases, you'll be able to improve their growing conditions for the next season, or you might just conclude that a certain plant just won't grow well in your climate.

Throughout the season, keep these harvesting tips in mind:

- If the flowers are the dye source, pick them throughout the season, whenever they're at full bloom.
- Pick berries whenever they're ripe.
- If you harvest an entire plant or the leaves, pick them at the end of the season when the dye content is at the peak.
- Most of the plants that contain dyes in their roots are perennial, so they will only have developed enough dye in them after two or three years.
- Keep the roots of biennial and perennial plants in the soil so they come back the next season.
- The parts of annual plants that weren't harvested for dyeing can be composted.

 **Annual versus Perennial**

An annual plant is a plant that only lives for one year/season; a biennial plant takes two years to complete its life cycle; and a perennial plant lives for more than two years.

# Extracting and Preparing the Dye

The first step in natural dyeing is extraction, followed by preparing a dye bath. Extract the dye from the materials in a pot or kettle large enough to fit your fibers or materials.

## EXTRACTING THE DYE

The extraction steps below apply to all kinds of natural dye sources, not just the ones listed.

### Dried Materials, including Roots and Hardwood Chips

1. Cut the materials into small pieces and/or pulverize them if needed. Soak the cut up bits in warm water overnight or at least 12 hours.
2. Add more water and bring the solution to a simmering temperature (or refer to the packaging instructions). Let it simmer for at least half an hour.
3. Strain the dye materials, saving the extracted liquid solution; this is the dye. The simmered dye materials can be saved and reused in future extractions.

### Fresh Materials

1. Chop the materials into small pieces and cover them with water. Bring the bath to a simmering temperature and let it simmer for at least half an hour.
2. Strain the dye material, saving the extract liquid solution. You can do a second extraction using the same dye material, but it won't be possible to dry it for future use.

### Extracts

Following the proportions recommended by the supplier, weigh the quantity of extract needed and add it to warm water, stirring until it is dissolved. Slowly raise the temperature to a simmering temperature.

## Dye Lab Safety Rules

- Use adequate protective material (gloves, aprons, goggles, respirator masks).
- Never leave a hot plate on unattended. Make sure you turn off the hot plates when you leave the room.
- Immediately clean any spill, especially if you are using a potentially harmful reagent (such as soda ash, urea water, etc.).
- Don't use the same measuring spoon or instrument in different reagent containers to avoid contamination.
- When throwing away large quantities of dye, mordant, fixative solution, etc., allow the water to run for an extended time.
- Label any dye/mordant/fixative solution that you are storing with your name, the date, and a description of the solution.
- Make sure to carefully read the safety sheets and/or packaging that come with the materials and reagents that you're using and keep them in a binder in the dye lab for reference.

## PREPARING THE DYE BATH

Once the dyes are extracted from the materials, the dye bath is ready. Simply add your fibers or yardage to the kettle or pot. Typically, you'll simmer the fibers for about thirty minutes or until they are the desired color. The longer you leave them in the dye bath, the deeper the color. The colors do tend to lighten once the fibers are dry, so to let the fibers soak longer if you want deeper colors. Dye baths can remain in the pot, or you can store them in plastic containers in the refrigerator for future use. Once they get moldy, you'll have to throw them away.

## The Dyeing Process

Before you dye your fibers, you need to scour (wash) them and then soak them in a mordant bath. Adjust the type of mordant, water temperature, and simmering time according to the type of fiber and the instructions on the mordant packaging.

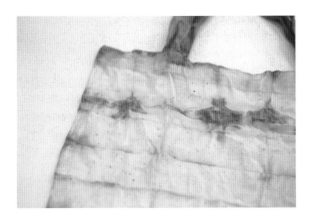

This naturally dyed tote bag can be made from instructions further on in this chapter.

## SCOURING THE FIBERS

First, you will need to scour, or wash your fibers. Scouring is essential to a good, even dye job, because it removes sizing or dirt from the fibers, allowing the dye to penetrate better. For wool, silk, and linen, wash the fibers in simmering (just below boiling) water with a few drops of pH neutral soap (synthrapol or any baby soap will work) for at least an hour. Wash cotton fibers in simmering water with a few drops of pH neutral soap and 2 teaspoons (10 g) of soda ash (or washing soda) per ounce of cotton for at least an hour.

Scouring is an important step in the dyeing process; it removes residue from the fabric that may stop dye from penetrating the fiber.

## MORDANTING THE FIBERS

Choose the best mordant for your project. The most popular mordant is aluminum, often called alum, because it is safe and easy to use and produces bright shades. When you are working with mordants, be sure to wear gloves, goggles, and a respirator, especially when the mordant powder is very fine.

Dissolve the mordant in warm water and add it to 2 gallons (7.6 L) of warm water. Refer to the instructions on the mordant for any specific instructions. Bring the water to the right temperature for the fiber type and immerse in the bath for about an hour. Refer to the instructions for how long to simmer the fibers. Let the water cool down and then rinse the fibers.

Shibori dyeing is a Japanese form of tie-dyeing. It has been used for a long time, but is also used today, as seen here in the work of Katrin Reifeiss.

## Dyeing Techniques

The most traditional dyeing technique is immersion dyeing, which involves simply immersing the fabric or yarn in a pot with the prepared dye bath and simmering it for about thirty minutes. This process produces a single color. There are several ways to vary the colors and the results (see resist dying in the project on page 134 and space dying in the project on page 136). Resist dyeing techniques, in which you restrict the areas of fabric or yarns that absorb the dye, are easy to do in a home studio. The resist is simply a substance or material that blocks the passage of the dye, preventing it from reaching the fiber. Some resist techniques, such as tie-dye and the Japanese Shibori, involve folding, creasing, and tying the fibers or fabric, and others, such as batik, involve the application of wax or starch-like pastes to create a designs.

## Tie-dye

Tie-dye involves folding, creasing, tying, and bundling fabric before dyeing. The parts of the fabric where it is folded, tied, and creased create resists to the penetration of the dye and therefore aren't dyed. Folds and creases create geometric patterns, while bundling and tying create more organic patterns. Any exterior element used to secure the folds, crease, and bundles, such as rubber bands, yarn, clamps, buttons, etc, will also be a resist and affect the final look.

Ancient examples of tie-dyed fabrics come from pre-Columbian cultures in Peru and date from 500 to 800 CE. Tie-dye also has a history in West Africa, especially with the use of indigo. India was (and is) known for using embroidery as the resist, especially for dyeing yarn that is then woven into a patterned fabric (called Ikat). However, it was Japan that perfected this technique as early as the eighth century BCE, under the name of Shibori.

## BATIK

Batik is a popular dyeing technique involving the use of wax or any other kind of paste resist applied to the fabric by painting, printing, or stamping. The fabric is then dyed in an immersion bath. After dyeing, the fabric is washed to remove the wax or paste. The areas covered by the wax won't be dyed because the wax prevented the dye from reaching the fabric. The fabric can be dyed again to add another color, often to the areas not previously dyed. Sometimes the areas dyed with the first immersion remain covered in wax so they don't get over-dyed other times the wax is removed so those areas can take dye. Batik is traditionally practiced in Indonesia, Malaysia, India, China, and Japan, with each country having developed its own traditional motifs and techniques.

## PAINTING OR PRINTING

Dyes can be applied directly to the surface of the fabric, by painting or printing, in order to create a specific design or pattern. In this case, a thickening substance, also called a print paste, is added to the dye solution to make it thicker. There are different substances used as thickeners, such as sodium alginate, arabic gum, gum tragacanth, etc. The thickener substance is mixed with warm water in a blender until it forms an even gel-like paste. You can control the thickness of the dye paste or paint by adding more or less thickener.

The dye powder, mordants, and/or other additives should be dissolved in a small amount of warm water and added to this paste, mixing all together well. When dye is applied in a topical way (instead of by immersion) like this, it needs to be steam-set to keep the color permanent and prevent it from bleeding. There are many ways you can steam-set fabric or yarn, either by using a pot steamer or a more complex stove top steamer. You can buy special equipment that comes with explicit instructions, or for small projects (1 yard [0.9 m] or less of fabric), you can use a standard double boiler. Don't submerge the fabric in water, just within the steam. Let the fabric steam for about an hour and then rinse and let it dry.

# Bag Tie-Dyed With Onion Skins

This project will guide you through the step-by-step process of dyeing a tote bag with onion skins. The skins of yellow onions contain dyes that will color all kinds of natural fibers in shades from yellow to orange. Of course, there's other stuff in your kitchen and garden that is just as much fun to experiment with, such as marigolds, rhubarb leaves, purple cabbage, and avocado skins. Follow the exact same process as described below and on the previous pages. You can also adapt this project to dye T-shirts, yarn, and fabric. Just adapt the quantities of mordant and dye to the weight of the project.

## EQUIPMENT

- Heat plate or stove top
- Measuring spoons
- Paring knife
- Safety gear (see page 130)
- Scale
- Stainless steel pot
- Tongs

## MATERIALS

- Aluminum sulfate/aluminum acetate (for mordant)
- Onions
- Rubber bands, pins, ties, etc. to hold folds in place
- pH neutral soap (synthrapol)
- Purchased tote bag
- Water

## INSTRUCTIONS

1. Weigh the tote bag before you wash it and make note of the weight. Wash the tote bag in the washing machine with hot water and a few drops of pH neutral soap for at least one hour. You can also wash it in a pot on your stove with a few drops of the same soap and allow it to simmer for one hour. Rinse well.

2. Put on your safety equipment and measure out the mordant. If you're using aluminum sulfate as your mordant, use 7–12% of the weight of the tote bag. If you're using aluminum acetate, the proportion should be 5–7% of the weight of the tote bag.

3. Dissolve the mordant in warm water and add it to 2 gallons (7.6 L) of water in the stainless steel pot. Bring the bath to a temperature around 180°F (82°C), just below boiling. Add the tote bag to the pot and let it simmer for about an hour, stirring occasionally.

4. After an hour, turn off the heat and let the bath cool with the tote bag in it. If possible, let the bag stay in the mordant bath overnight to help the mordant bond with the fibers. Rinse the bag thoroughly in clean water.

5. You can get creative and try any kind of tying, folding, twisting, or pleating. The bag shown was folded into accordion pleats and held closed with rubber bands. The idea is to prevent some areas from getting dyed, so make sure you tie, pin, or sew your resist tightly **[A, B, C]**.

6. Remove the onion skins from the onions, put about two handfuls of them into a stainless steel pot, and cover them with water **[D, E]**. Simmer the onion skins for about a half hour. You'll notice the water becomes a golden reddish color. Remove the onion skins and save the liquid. You can discard the onion skins or dry and save them because they'll still have some dye and can be reused.

7. Keep the bath in the stainless steel pot and add the mordanted tote bag **[F]**. Add more water as needed so the bag can move freely in the dye bath. Let the tote bag simmer for 30–40 minutes. Then, turn off the heat and let the bag cool. Once cool, rinse the bag with pH-neutral soap and water.

8. Remove the rubber bands, ties, or whatever you used to hold the folds **[G, H]**. Allow the bag to dry, and you are all set!

# PROJECT:
# Space-Dyed Yarn

Space dyeing is a technique that gives yarn or fabric a mottled, multicolored effect. When you knit, crochet, or weave with space-dyed yarn, you can create colored patterns without having to change yarn. We suggest using two color dyes, but you can use as many as you want; just repeat the procedure described below.

## EQUIPMENT

- Measuring cups and spoons
- Niddy noddy (optional)
- Plastic container, sized so it holds the yarn or fabric snugly
- Saran wrap or plastic bag

## MATERIALS

- Cotton yarn (3.5 oz [98 g])
- Dye activator (soda ash)
- Two colors of fiber reactive dyes (Procion MX)
- pH-neutral soap

## EQUIPMENT

1. Wind your cotton thread/yarn into a skein using a niddy noddy (see page 61) or by winding it around your forearm. Use a piece of yarn to tie the skein together loosely in several places to prevent it from coming undone.

2. Soak the yarn in warm water with a drop of pH-neutral soap for about thirty minutes. This process opens the fibers and allows for better penetration of the dye.

3. For this project, we used two different color fiber reactive dyes (Procion MX), pink and blue, but you can use as many dyes as you wish. Prepare 1 cup (235 ml) of dyeing solution for each color by dissolving the dye powder in 1 cup (235 ml) of warm water.

### Common Natural Dyes

|  | PALE | MEDIUM | DARK |
|---|---|---|---|
| **DYE POWDER** | ½ teaspoon or less | 1 to 2 teaspoons (5 to 10 g) | 3 to 5 teaspoons (15 to 50 g) |

4. Place the damp skein (or fabric) in the plastic container; it should fit snugly. Fold, crease, and twist the yarn as desired **[A]**.

A

B

C

D

5. Pour the two dye solutions slowly over the yarn, allowing the fibers to absorb them **[B]**. You don't want the yarn totally submerged in the dye solution for this technique or it won't create the mottled effects that you expect of space-dyed yarn. Note that you might not need or desire to use all the dye solution. You can also experiment manipulating the yarn and/or pressing it down after applying the dye. Pressing on the fibers will make the colors blend together, whereas if you don't touch them, there will be a clearer distinction between the two colors.

6. Once you're happy with the dyeing and color saturation, let the yarn sit for about 15–30 minutes.

7. While you're waiting, prepare the dye activator solution by dissolving 2 teaspoons (10 g) of soda ash in 1 cup (235 ml) of water.

8. Once the fibers have sat for 15–30 minutes, pour the dye activator solution over them **[C]**. Cover the yarn (or fabric) with a plastic bag or plastic wrap and let it sit for at least four hours or as long as you can (24 hours is recommended) so the fixing action occurs **[D]**.

9. Rinse the yarn thoroughly with warm water and pH neutral soap.

10. Allow the skein to dry, and then wind it into a ball of yarn. You can use a swift and ball winder or go to a yarn shop where they will do it for you. Then it's ready to use!

# Sewing, Quilting, and Appliqué

Fundamentally, sewing is a technique that binds materials together for construction and decoration. It is the basis for many textile processes, such as quilting, embroidery, appliqué, beading, and tapestry. Before you can quilt or appliqué, you need to know the basics of hand sewing, and of course, for speed and ease it's nice to know how to sew by machine. Sewing is a difficult topic to cover in only one chapter, but we're happy to get you started and interested in one of the oldest and easiest of the textile media.

## A Brief History of Sewing

Like most textile media, it is difficult to say exactly when the techniques originated, but archeologists believe sewing developed in its simplest stages during the prehistoric Paleolithic era. Needles were formed from bone and animal sinew, while veins and intestine were used for thread.

Hand sewing is worked with a needle and thread and employs several basic stitches, such as the running stitch, basting stitch, whipstitch, and backstitch. Hand sewing can be a painstaking and laborious practice, but it is a very useful skill, especially for mending and tailoring. Prior to the invention of the sewing machine in the nineteenth century, clothing and home décor goods were sewn by hand. Today, hand sewing and tailoring is the mark of high quality goods.

The tools for sewing, quilting and applique are many and are small (and inexpensive), so this is where good organization and storage comes in handy.

Machine sewing is definitely faster than hand sewing and a quality sewing machine is a good investment and relatively inexpensive. With the invention of the sewing machine during the Industrial Revolution, the garment and textile industry changed dramatically, allowing for the mass production of clothing and other goods. Sewing machines also became a staple in many households. The first sewing machine patent was issued to Thomas Saint in 1790, but it is not known whether a prototype was ever created. Many other patents were awarded, but nothing was truly successful until Isaac Singer's lockstitch machine. Although Singer is the name associated with the invention of the sewing machine, Walter Hunt was the first inventor of the lockstitch machine, but he never patented the idea because he believed the machine would lead to unemployment! Elias Howe was the first to patent the machine, and he later got into "patent wars" with Isaac Singer. Howe earned several million dollars from patent royalties after winning his case against Singer. Today there are many types of sewing machines, including computerized models that stitch beautiful embroidery and several novelty construction stitches.

Again, sewing is worthy of its own book, but in this chapter, you'll learn basic hand stitches and how to sew a seam on a sewing machine. From there, garment construction, quilt work, and appliqué are only a step away.

# Equipping Your Studio

Whether you sew now and again to finish other forms of textile media or it is your main process, we recommend equipping your studio with the following items:

### Home Sewing Machine

- Machine, sewing, and embroidery needles in different sizes
- Bobbins
- Iron and ironing board
- Variety of sewing thread
- Dressmaker straight pins (lots of them!)
- Pin Cushion
- Fabric scissors (that you use for fabric ONLY)
- Seam ripper
- Tape measure
- Tailor's chalk or fabric marking pens
- Yardstick

### For Quilting:

- Rotary cutter
- Clear rulers
- Cutting mat

### Optional, but nice to have:

- Serger
- Thread stand or other good thread storage
- Dress form (for garment construction)
- Quilting frame

If you plan to quilt or construct clothing, you will need ample table space, preferably with a padded surface (see project page 26). Whether you use commercial sewing patterns or a dress form to drape and create your own patterns, you'll need room! Sewing is really the transformation of two-dimensional fabric into a three-dimensional garment, toy, drapery, or just about anything made from textiles.

## THE SEWING MACHINE

The sewing machine was invented for speed and efficiency and can do amazing things. Of course, very detailed work and precise pattern matching is best done by hand, but almost everything else can be done on a basic sewing machine that can execute a straight, reverse, and zigzag stitch. Be sure to review the instruction manual to understand how your machine works.

Even the most basic sewing machines will have these important features:

- Power switch
- Foot, knee, or touch pad control to start and stop the machine
- Bobbins and bobbin winder (You'll want to wind different color threads onto a selection of bobbins. The bobbin sits below the needle and presser foot in the bobbin case.)
- A needle that lowers and rises to create stitches
- Several presser feet come with a sewing machine, usually a general-purpose foot, a straight stitch foot, and a zipper foot. The presser foot keeps the fabric in place while the feed dogs (on the base of the sewing machine) move the fabric forward.
- Thread spool pin and thread guides to hold the upper (or needle) thread—there will also be a threading guide printed on the machine or illustrated in the manual. It is very important for the thread to follow the correct path.
- Tension and stitch regulators or dials that you adjust to change the thread tension, stitch type, stitch length, and stitch width
- Reverse stitch button or dial
- Balance wheel, which turns as your needle moves up and down—you can use the wheel to manually control your needle.

With a sewing machine, there are two threads (as opposed to sewing by hand, which uses only one thread): the needle thread and the bobbin thread. The two threads interlock between the fabric layers. The key to successful sewing is knowing how to work your machine, so keep the instruction manual handy.

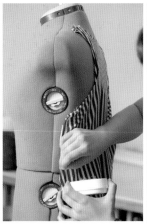

**LEFT** Draping is the method of creating a garment by tucking, pinning, and pleating fabric over a dress form to sculpt a garment.

**RIGHT** Shown here is a serger, which can be used to finish edges.

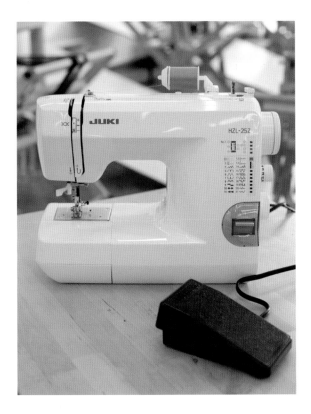

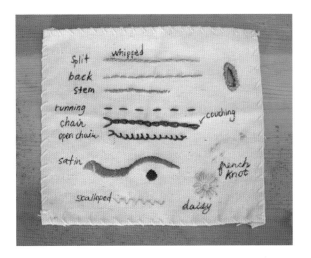

## Storage

You will need storage for fabric because all sewers hoard fabric! It needs to be far away from the wet area of your studio. You'll also need containers and labels. The tools needed are few, but they are small and should be kept in labeled drawers, tins, boxes, and the like. Whatever storage method you choose, it just needs to be organized! Revisit chapter one (page 19) for some pointers on organization.

## The Basics of Hand Sewing

To stitch by hand, simply thread a hand needle with an 18 inches (45.7 cm) length of thread and knot one end. Keep your stitches uniform in size and don't pull the thread too tight or leave it too loose. Knowledge of the following four stitches will allow you to do any hand sewing, but there are many more that you can learn over time. Some of the following are also used in embroidery and for decorative stitching.

## Straight or Running Stitch

A straight or running stitch is basic for hand sewing. It is the quintessential stitch formed in equal lengths either for construction or for decoration.

## Basting Stitch

A basting stitch is a very long, loose straight stitch used to hold something in place temporarily. Use it to quickly stitch something together to see what it will look like. It's easy to remove the stitches by snipping and pulling the thread. A basting stitch can also be used to gather fabric.

## Whipstitch

A whipstitch (also known as a blanket stitch) is used for binding or finishing edges. You can finish a single edge of fabric or bind two edges together because the thread wraps around the fabric edge(s).

## Backstitch

The backstitch is a stitch that looks like one continuous line, with no breaks (unlike the straight stitch, which has breaks). It is used for embroidering or decorative stitching, finishing, and because it is such a strong stitch, for construction.

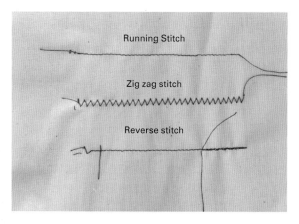

Depending on your home sewing machine, you can create a number of intricate stitches. Running, zig zag, and reverse stitches are standard to any machine and have specific uses that make your sewing better.

## The Basics of Machine Sewing

As long as you can sew a straight stitch forward and in reverse and a stretch stitch, you can sew anything.

## Straight Stitch

The straight stitch is used to sew woven fabrics. Adjust the length of the stitch for temporary (basting) stitches or for construction stitches, which are typically shorter than basting stitches.

## Reverse Stitch

By sewing in reverse at the beginning and end of a seam, you lock the stitches so they don't pull out or come undone. Every machine has a button, lever, or dial that instructs the machine to sew in reverse.

## Zigzag Stitch

Another basic stitch common to almost all sewing machines, the zigzag is used for edge finishing and for sewing knit fabrics. The stitch has built-in stretch, so it is ideal when working with fabrics that stretch.

## Sewing a Plain Seam

1. Raise the needle to the highest position and lift the presser foot. Position the fabric layers, with the raw edges aligned, under the presser foot so the cut edges align with the ½" (1.3 cm) or ⅝" (1.6 cm) seam allowance markings on the bed of the machine. The width of the seam allowances depends on the project and the instructions usually indicate the appropriate seam allowance width.
2. Lower the presser foot and hold the threads out behind the needle. Take two or three stitches and adjust the machine to sew two or three stitches in reverse. Backstitch to the edge of the fabric and switch the machine to stitch forward again.
3. Continue stitching, with the cut edges along the seam allowance marking, to the end of the seam. Backstitch again for about ½" (1.3 cm). Raise the presser foot and pull the fabric out. Cut the threads to remove the fabric.
4. Press the seam and trim the seam allowances.

# Tutorial: French Seams

French seams are specialty seams, perfect for delicate fabrics that unravel easily and for times when you don't want to see the seam allowances. It is an enclosed seam and a professional way to finish the raw edges inside the garment or project.

## TOOLS

- Sewing machine
- Straight pins
- Sharp fabric scissors
- Iron and ironing board

## MATERIALS

- Fabric and matching thread

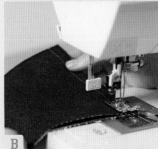

## INSTRUCTIONS:

1. Press the fabric with the iron set on a heat setting appropriate for the fiber content (high for cottons, low for silks, etc).

2. Pin the fabric layers with the wrong sides together, and sew them together with ½" (1.3 cm) seam allowances (see page 140). **[A, B]**

3. Trim the seam allowances close to the seam to about ⅛" (3 mm). Trim the threads as well. Use sharp fabric scissors so that the cut edge is very clean and threads are not snagged. **[C, D]**

This Singer home machine is a great one to learn on, but you can also keep it for years to come and advance your skills with it. A good machine is a very worthwhile investment.

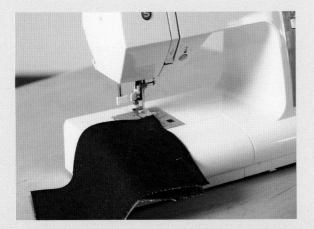

4. Open the seam and press the seam allowance to one side and then fold the right sides together, enclosing the trimmed seam allowances. **[E, F]**

5. Stitch a second seam with the right sides together. Stitch as close to the edge as possible without sewing over the encased edges. The point of this technique is to encase the raw edges within the seam. **[G]**

6. Remove the fabric from the machine, and you will see that it looks very neat on both sides. The right side looks normal and the wrong side has a completely enclosed edge. You will immediately see whether you fully encased the raw edge or not, because if you didn't, little threads from the cut edges will poke through the seam on the right side. As you practice, you will get more comfortable with the technique and quickly eliminate visible threads. **[H]**

---

### TIP Neat Seams

If you have visible threads on the right side of a French seam, it means the second seam was stitched too close to the folded edge. Next time, make that second line of stitching a bit farther from the edge.

## The Basics of Quilting

Traditionally, quilts serve as practical and beautiful elements for the home. American quilting traditions began with the need to salvage fabrics when clothing or bed linens tore or became too worn. Small scraps were patch-worked together to create a new textile, with patterns and images created through collage. Because quilts, especially when done completely by hand, were (and still are) so labor intensive, they were often made for commemorative purposes such as weddings, births, deaths, and other major life events.

A quilt is a type of blanket that consists of two fabric layers with a layer of batting between. The layers are sewn together and the edges are bound by sewing with a strip of fabric or binding. Quilts generally have an element of patchwork, applique, or imagery on the top layer, while the back layer is often a plain fabric.

Quilting is simply holding together at least two layers of fabric with stitches. Often there is a middle layer that acts as insulation, but a fabric can also be quilted to something else.

## The Basics of Appliqué

Appliqué is an exciting way to introduce design interest by layering small patches or shapes on a garment, accessory, table linen, or just about anything. It is the technique of superimposing shapes on a ground cloth. The process is suitable for all types of fabric; you can use lightweight fabrics such as cottons and silk or heavier ones such as corduroy, denim, and even leather! All you need to appliqué is a needle and thread, scissors, swatches of fabric, the item to be appliquéd, a small table or workstation, and a little imagination.

## Appliqué Inspiration

There is no limit to what you can do, as long as the background fabric can support the appliqué. Avoid using heavy fabric appliqués on sheer and lightweight fabrics, although you can certainly use any fabrics, even gauze, on heavier fabrics.

- When used sparingly, applique is a way to ornament a specific area. Use it to draw attention to a collar, cuff, or pocket.
- An appliqué cut from silk, velvet, or other luxurious fabric can give the impression of a piece of jewelry.
- Layer multiple shapes of fabric just as you would use paper to create a collage.
- Experiment with reverse appliqué. Instead of cutting out a red circle and patching it on top of a blue tote, try cutting a circle out of the blue tote, positioning a red swatch under the hole, and stitching around the hole through both layers. To keep the opening neat, turn under the edges in the blue cloth.
- The type of stitch you use to attach the appliques will affect the look of the final piece, so explore various embroidery stitches (see chapter 9).
- Consider adding beading, sequins, and other decorative trims to your project. A border of seed beads adds dimension and a subtle sparkle.

# Tutorial: Easy Patchwork Quilting

You won't need many materials other than fabric, needles, thread, and batting. Some work can be done on the sewing machine and some by hand.

## INSTRUCTIONS:

1. A popular quilt is one made with scraps of fabric that are sewn together, often called a patchwork quilt. Choose fabrics that work well together and cut them into square pieces; you decide the size.

2. Machine stitch (or hand sew) the squares with the right sides together to create the top layer **[A]**. This will take some planning to obtain the desired size.

3. Lay out your quilt layers with the bottom layer right side down, then the batting, and finally the top layer with the right side up. Pin the layers together **[B]**.

4. After layering your top, batting, and backing, this is where you normally would tack and stitch by hand. If you are just placing simple tacks within the quilt to secure the pieces, you don't need a quilting frame **[C]**. But if you are using embroidery stitches or applique to quilt the pieces together, a quilting frame will help keep the pieces taut. This is similar to the idea of an embroidery hoop, but is usually much larger.

5. Once you have stitched your batting together, you can use a sewing machine to tack them permanently in any configuration you like. **[D]** Here we do straight lines going in both directions, spaced unevenly. After you are done, you can removing the tacking stitches. **[E]** If you were to use this fabric to make something else (a pillow, for example), you would continue on. If you were making a quilt, you would finish the edges with a binding.

A

B

C

D

E

> **TIP**  ## Crazy Quilt
>
> Some quilts, like the Crazy Quilts of Gees Bend, are made with irregular shapes and take on a more organic shape. There are hundreds of cultural, traditional, and contemporary patterns to explore and learn about!

# Mending with Reverse Appliqué

Use appliqués to extend the life of some of your favorite items. The jacket in this project had a tear in the sleeve, so a well-placed appliqué made it ready for wearing.

## TOOLS

- Paper and pencil
- Paper and fabric scissors
- Tailor's chalk or fabric marking pen
- Straight pins
- Hand-sewing needle

## MATERIALS

- Item to be mended
- 1 piece of heavy-weight red cotton, about 5" x 8" (12.7 x 20.3 cm)
- 1 piece of light-weight batting about 5" x 8" (12.7 x 20.3 cm)
- 1 piece of light-weight blue cotton about 5" x 8" (12.7 x 20.3 cm)
- Blue or red thread

Appliqué is a great way to mend clothing. It's a simple and easy way to get creative, so before you throw out a good garment or fabric item, think about what you could apply to it to mend it and use it further. This comes in very handy with kids.

## INSTRUCTIONS

1. Smooth out the item on your work surface. Close all buttons or zippers so you can assess the size of the hole or tear.

2. Slide the paper under the tear or hole and trace the hole onto the paper to the approximate size area you need to cover. Pull out the paper and draw a heart (or any shape) around the traced marks. **[A, B]**

3. Cut the heart shape out of the paper and use it as a template. Position the paper template over the tear and trace around it with tailor's chalk or a disappearing ink fabric marker. **[C]**

4. Cut directly on the traced outline, leaving a heart-shaped hole where the tear used to be. **[D]**

5. Layer the fabrics, red fabric right side down, batting, and blue fabric wrong side down and trim them to desired size to completely cover the heart-shaped hole with at least 1 inch (2.5 cm) extra all around. Baste the layers together.

6. Turn the jacket sleeve wrong side out. Center and pin the fabric layers under the heart-shaped hole. Baste or pin the layers to the jacket. **[E]**

7. Turn the jacket right side out and pin the cut edges of the heart-shaped hole to the wrong side. **[F]**

8. Handsew around the folded edges, through all the layers, using red or blue thread. **[G]** A straight stitch (page 142) or blanket stitch (page 155) works best.

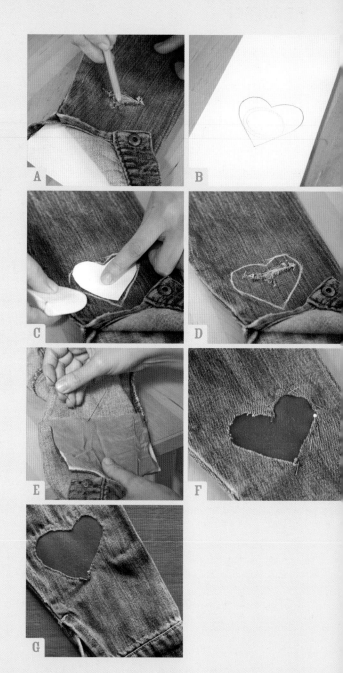

# Drawstring Bag

Sewing is the basis for many other needle arts. The sewing instructions for a very simple drawstring bag follow, but consider first making patchwork fabric and using it to make the bag, or appliquéing unique shapes onto a very plain fabric to incorporate multiple techniques into one fabulous project. You can even sew French seams!

Practice sewing with very simple projects like this drawstring bag to perfect basic sewing principles. As you advance your skills, you'll find that much of sewing is common sense and an ability to envision how to transform flat fabric into something three-dimensional.

## TOOLS

- Sewing machine
- Iron and ironing board
- Straight pins
- Fabric scissors
- Safety pin

## MATERIALS

- 2 pieces of fabric each 10" x 12" (25.4 x 30.5 cm), or any size of your choice
- 2 yards (1.8 m) of ribbon, cord, or string for the drawstring

The drawstring bag pattern can be used over and over and altered or embellished. Getting comfortable with simple patterns like this and then changing them according to your own desire is a great way to practice sewing and construction principles.

# INSTRUCTIONS

1. Thread your sewing machine with the color of your choice. The thread will be visible at the top of the bag, so if you want contrast, use a thread color different from the fabric. But if you want the thread to blend in, choose a thread color that is close to the fabric color (the background of the fabric if it is patterned). It is best to use the same top and bobbin threads, but if you don't, remember that the bobbin color appears on the bottom layer.

2. Press the fabric and then cut two pieces each 10 x 12 inches (25.4 x 30.5 cm), or to the desired size. Fold one 10" (25.4 cm) edge of each piece 1½ inches (3.8 cm) to the wrong side and press. **[A, B]**

3. To make the drawstring casing, machine stitch the fold in place along the cut edge, not the folded edge. Don't stitch the sides. **[C]**

4. Pin the two pieces with the right sides together and both stitched edges at the top.

5. Machine stitch the unfinished three sides of the bag ½ inch (1.3 cm) from the raw edges. Start the seam just below the casing seam on the right edge of the bag (about 1 inch [2.5 cm] from the top). Reverse stitch at the start of the seam and sew down to ½ inch (1.3 cm) from the bottom edge. With the needle down, lift the presser foot and pivot the fabric (or rotate the fabric 90 degrees). Continue stitching across the bottom. **[D, E, F, G, H]**

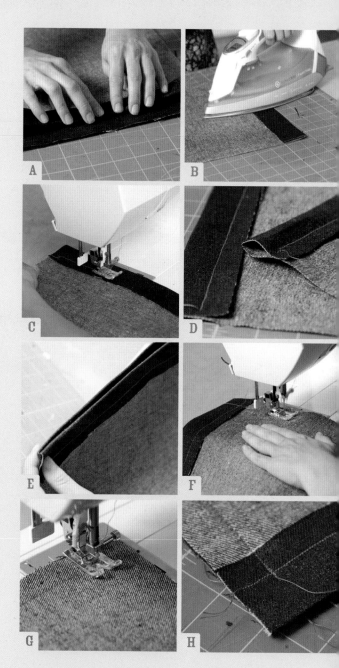

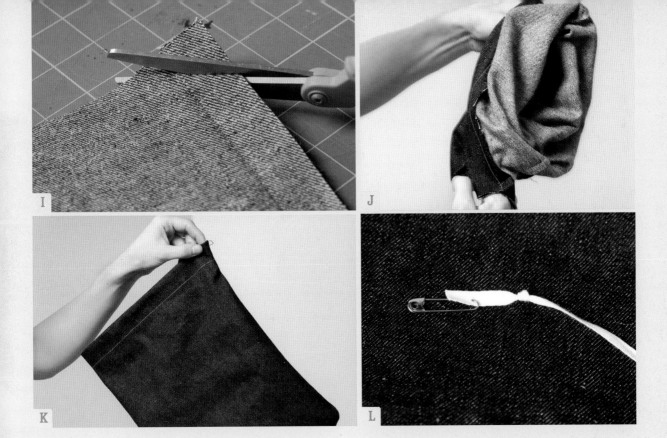

6. Repeat when you get to the next corner and stitch up the last side. Stop stitching about 1 inch (2.5 cm) from the top edge, at the casing stitching, and reverse stitch. Cut the threads and remove the fabric from the machine.

7. Trim the seam allowances close to the stitching and trim the corners diagonally as shown. Trimming the corners will reduce bulk at the corners when you turn the bag right side out. **[I]**

8. Turn the bag right side out and push out the corners. Press. **[J, K]**

9. Cut the drawstring or ribbon into two pieces. Pin a safety pin to one end of one piece and insert in one casing opening. Use the safety pin to work the end of the drawstring through the casing. Repeat with the remaining drawstring through the other casing. Tie the drawstring ends together and then slide the drawstring through the casings so the knots are hidden. You're all set! **[L]**

TIP | **Using Zigzag Stitch**

If the fabric tends to ravel, you might want to finish the edges by overcast stitching or zigzag stitch all the cut edges before you start the construction process, or you can use pinking shears.

# Needlework

**Needlework is a broad category describing a number of needle and thread techniques used to decorate or reinforce fabric.** The application of embellishment is wide and diverse and is not only limited to hand work but can be done using sewing and embroidery machines. You may choose to equip your home studio with one of these, or you may prefer to use a traditional embroidery hoop to keep your fabric taut while you decorate the surface by hand. Because it is such a natural means toward personalizing fabric, these are some of the oldest techniques in the textile arts, and ones that have a cultural value as well as an artistic one. Much can be gleaned about a people by their clothing and in particular, about the way in which the clothing is embellished, personalized, and mended. For example, in ancient Greece, Rome, and China, stitching was often symbolic and done in gold silk thread on religious and royal robes. Fabric embellishments such as beading were also used to indicate victories in battle, much like we use medals today. On the other hand, during frugal time periods, such as the Colonial period of America and the Great Depression, stitching was done to reinforce cloth and extend its life.

Since the Industrial Revolution, we have had a different relationship to mending and embellishment. The mechanization of various industries including textiles brought a whole new approach to the production of fabric. Many could suddenly afford items such as clothing and home furnishings that were before reserved for the wealthy because the textile mill chugging away replaced the painstaking effort of the craftsman. This meant a higher standard of living for the masses but also a blow to the uniqueness of each garment produced. The greater good of clothing the poor won out, but the longing for the high quality and attention to detail of handmade clothing never died. There is so much that we as individuals feel for our garments, our favorite sweaters, our "boyfriend jeans," hand-me-downs, and secondhand clothes, that extends way beyond practical body covering. It is a way in which we present ourselves and express our tastes, ambitions, and associations or a lack thereof. The desire to personalize clothing has driven many fashion trends and reflects the mood of the times.

As many remember, in the 1970s, embroidery and other textile surface embellishment techniques enjoyed a rich revival. It served as a reminder of times when the individual was valued more highly than the collectivism of the WWII era, and subsequent commercialism of the Baby Boom generation, and the military atmosphere surrounding the Korean and Vietnam wars allowed. The resulting look was reminiscent of traditional and folk clothing from around the world—a commentary on the value of the individual as well as the value of cultural diversity and racial equality. As a political and emotional expression of a generation's frustration with conformity, the vibrant, embellished look was a joyful rebellion against the uniformity that is associated with mass-produced fabric. The personalized, politicized clothing and long unrestrained hair made a natural reference to the social fabric of the time. Every piece of clothing that is stitched, patched, embroidered, or printed by hand is a unique garment, as unique as its wearer, and like hand-formed stitches, perfect in its imperfection.

The power of expression that embellishment gives the maker is considerable, whatever the statement may be. Making a personal mark on a garment can bring meaning and increased personal value even to the most mundane domestic article. Monograms serve a personalizing function beyond helping to identify the owner of the item. The close attention required to execute small even stitches bestow a perceived value to the embroidered object by implying an investment of time and energy on behalf of the embroiderer. Traditional dowry items include embroidered and embellished bed and table linens and clothing and serve as a testament of the virtue of the bride as a homemaker, as well as a woman. They are unarguable proofs of self-discipline and patience—one may say they are proofs of moral fiber.

This effect may be somewhat diminished in modern times because of the existence of sewing machines that produce embroidery. However, the look of machine embroidery will never totally replace handwork because the absolute regularity and uniformity of the stitches will always betray the work of a machine. While many an embroiderer strives for perfection, what may be seen as irregularity is often where the beauty lies for the viewer. There is so much to admire in the hard work that is handwork that the machine can never claim.

Wherever you find inspiration, you will enjoy practicing and exploring the needlework techniques described in this chapter. They all add interest and ornamentation, and many add delicacy and a sense of tradition to clothing, accessories, home décor, and fine art projects.

# Equipping Your Studio

One of the beautiful things about handmade needle-work is that you need very few tools. It's a good idea to keep an assortment of embroidery threads and needles in your studio because you'll find you reach for them for all kinds of quick embellishments.

- Several cuts of woven fabric, some even weave for counted stitching
- Embroidery needles in a variety of sizes
- Several weight, color, and fiber varieties of thread or embroidery floss
- Embroidery hoop
- Washable fabric marker
- Scissors

## CHOOSING A MACHINE

When choosing equipment for your home studio, you may go for a sewing machine that you will use to embroider. By moving the fabric under the foot, you can create "drawings" with the stitches, changing colors for added interest, or pleating the fabric for a three-dimensional effect. You may also use any of the various stitches that your machine can make. On some sewing machines, the stitches available are limited to straight stitch and zigzag, but on others, the options may be quite abundant and include shapes and designs to make you marvel.

The technology you choose has a lot to do with what your intended use is. If you would like to make embroidered caps, totes, or t-shirts, an embroidery machine is what you want. These have multiple needles, even multiple heads, and are programmable and capable of automatic color change. Many embroidery machines come with patterns that you can select with the press of a button to see the image appear in seconds, but they do not come cheap. They are indispensable if you need to be able to create identical items again and again. But as with a lot of industrial equipment, you may have to consider the electrical usage and even whether the machine will fit through your studio door.

# Types of Needlework

The fundamentals of most decorative hand stitching are the same as they were hundreds of years ago; the creative element is in the mixing of stitches, threads, designs, and foundation fabrics. This handcraft is truly in your hands.

There are many books out there that highlight needle work artists, techniques and projects. Both *Hoopla* by Leanne Praine and *PUSH: Stitchery* by Jamie Chalmers are great examples for inspiration and further information on needle work.

## EMBROIDERY

Embroidery is the art of stitching with thread on top of, or through, a foundation fabric to create surface designs. It is the closest a textile artist can come to drawing. It's a captivating way to add text and representational imagery to woven cloth. You can design your own stitch patterns, or there are numerous patterns for embroidering clothing, bedding, and accessories in books and magazines.

You can embroider any fabric, including unwoven materials such as felt, paper, plastics, and lightweight leather. However, the threads in even-weave fabrics provide a grid that can be used to guide the size and regularity of stitches through a technique known as counted-thread embroidery. The most popular form of counted stitching is cross stitch, which is a great first stitch to learn. Often counted stitching is pre-stamped on even-weave fabrics, making it perfect for beginners. At the other end of the embroidery spectrum is free embroidery, which relies on a foundation fabric for support, but doesn't require positioning stitches on or between threads. Free embroidery can be done with a sewing machine or by hand.

Shown at right are some of the most widely used embroidery stitches.

Chain Stitch

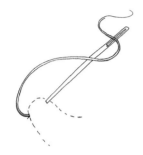

Satin Stitch

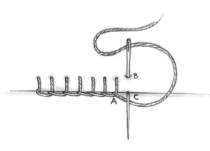

Blanket Stitch

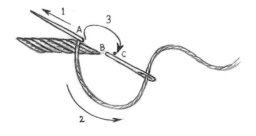

Stem Stitch

**Chain Stitch** The chain stitch is a basic embroidery stitch with a flowing linked line. It does not require the needle to pass through more than one layer of fabric. It can be used to outline or fill in areas.

**Satin Stitch** Sometimes called a damask stitch, the satin stitch is used to completely cover the ground fabric with a series of flat, straight stitches placed close together.

**Cross Stitch** The cross stitch is formed in the shape of an "x", or "+" on even-weave fabric (see page 156). It's one of the oldest and most widely used stitches across the world.

**Blanket Stitch** Used for finishing edges, attaching appliqués, and making hand-worked buttonholes, the blanket stitch is sometimes called the whipstitch or buttonhole stitch. It looks like a straight line with stitches radiating from it and can also be used on the surface of a fabric to create decorative designs.

**Couching** Couching, or laid work, creates a three-dimensional texture by fastening a yarn or cord on the surface of fabric with small stitches of the same color, but lighter-weight thread.

**Backstitch** Backstitch, also referred to in the sewing chapter, is a great stitch because it forms a single, thin continuous line, so it makes a great drawing tool for embroidery. To create this stitch, form a straight stitch but begin the next stitch back at the last stitch so that there are no spaces.

**Stem Stitch** Work a stem stitch from left to right, taking regular small stitches along the line of the design you are embroidering. The thread always comes up in the fabric on the left side of the last stitch. You can use this to outline designs, make flower stems, or even fill in areas.

## CREWELWORK

Crewelwork is a kind of free embroidery that produces a varied and intricate surface through the laying down of stitches side by side. As with other kinds of free embroidery, the stitches are not dependent on the woven grid in the ground cloth. The pattern is based on embroidering stitches in different sizes and directions to create a continuous color field. By changing the direction of the stitches, the embroiderer changes the angle at which the light reflects off the thread. That in turn alters the shade of the color a little bit. This subtle change can offer a rich and sophisticated feel to the finished piece without using more than three or four different stitches. Crewelwork is most effective with silk thread (as was done traditionally in China), but you can use wool and cotton yarns as well. To appreciate the full range of possibilities, you only need master the most familiar stitches. Most commonly, crewelwork is comprised of patterning done with the satin stitch, backstitch, stem stitch, and chain stitch.

## CROSS STITCH

Cross stitch is named for the "X" stitch formed when two straight stitches are crossed. This single embroidery stitch has become a particular technique in itself. If you like the look of traditional Scandinavian textiles or textiles from the Greek Islands, you will love cross stitch. It is precise and meticulous work with the pattern often preprinted on woven cotton or linen cloth (with warp and weft forming a grid) and the colors blocked off. To make the stitches the same length, the embroiderer counts the number of threads in the background fabric. Because of the regularity of the stitching, both sides of the fabric look the same, making the fabric reversible. The stitch itself can morph, changing the crossing angle to form other stitches such as the herringbone stitch, but the crossing pattern remains consistent.

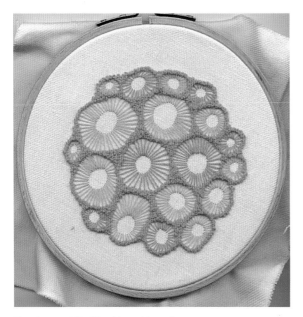

Though a very old traditional form of decorative embroidery, there are contemporary artists such as Katherine Shaughnessy who have applied the crewelwork technique to more contemporary work.

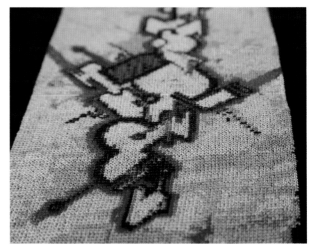

Cross stitch is another form of using thread to draw. In cross stitch, stitches are regular and even, and the fabric is reversible. Shown here is the work of Jamie Chalmers, aka Mr X Stitch, a very popular UK-based artist.

## OPENWORK

Sometimes called needle weaving or white work because it is often done on a white ground with white thread, openwork refers to all embroidery that looks like lace but is really stitching on fabric. This kind of needlework is very old and has a deep history in Scandinavian textile art. This technique requires precision to remove specific threads from the ground fabric to form open spaces or holes. Once a regular pattern is established, the holes are rimmed with embroidery stitches to create the appearance of lace. Openwork is traditionally applied to table linens and bedding as borders, but can be used anywhere to create an open structure.

## CUTWORK

If you like the look of open spaces in cloth, you can also try the technique called cutwork, or broderie angaise. This technique removes more of the ground cloth than openwork and is often found in decorative cuffs on clothing and high-end bed- and table linens.

To do cutwork, regular embroidery stitches are worked in patterns before any cloth is cut away. The result is a highly intricate and frilly fabric, like the one often seen in collars and cuffs in the sixteenth-century Spanish court.

## Drawn-Thread Work

If you don't like the idea of cutting out background threads, you can experiment with drawn-thread work. This technique creates open spaces that are lace-like, but the ground cloth stays intact. The spaces are achieved through a pulling apart threads and securing them in a pattern with embroidery stitches. Nothing is cut, so that the edges of the holes are a little bit thicker than those in openwork and cutwork.

## BEADING

Decorative beading is a means of adding sparkle and texture to fabrics and other accessories. It was traditionally done with glass, wood, or animal bone beads and other natural materials, but has greatly expanded today to include many more materials such as synthetics. Beading can be done through on- and off-loom weaving, stringing, sewing, gluing, embroidery, knitting, and crochet. Every form of textile media can benefit from a sparkle or two.

There is some difference in the appearance of beads that have been applied to the fiber before it is woven, knitted, or fully constructed and the look of beads that are sewn or glued on later. The latter will have a more pronounced dimensionality and may be more vulnerable to damage through wear and use of the cloth because they lie atop the fabric rather than integrated into the fabric construction.

# Embroidered Note Cards

Here's an easy way to incorporate embroidery into your greeting cards. You know that the cards are displayed on the mantle, the desk, the piano, or the fridge, so delight your family and friends with handmade cards that are worth showing off. Depending on the stitch, the cards may have a comforting and old time feeling, or be as modern and sharp as graphic art. Experiment with the kind of thread you use; try metallic thread on dark paper or fuzzy yarns on a patterned card. Whatever you do, you can be sure that your cards stand out from the rest.

## TOOLS

- Paper
- Pencil
- Embroidery needle
- Regular sewing needle
- Towel (optional)

## MATERIALS

- Thread or embroidery floss
- Blank cards

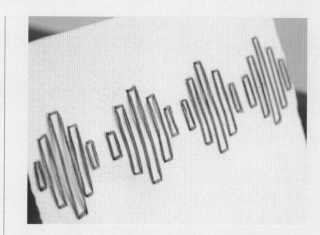

## INSTRUCTIONS

1. Draw out your design on paper. It can be a simple line drawing because once you start the embroidery it will come to life. **[A]**

2. Work on a padded surface (see how to make a padded surface on page 26). If you don't have a padded surface, simply place a folded towel on your table. Position the paper on top of the card so that the drawing is directly over the desired location for the embroidery. If you are using a folded card, open it so it is flat on the work surface.

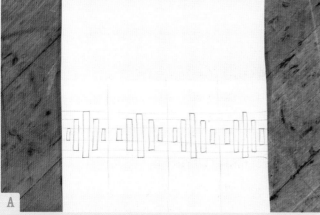

A

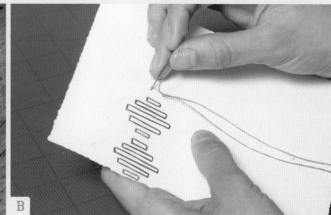

B

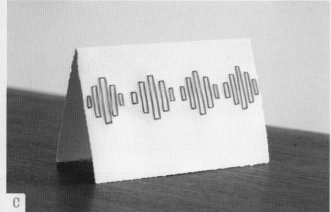

C

3. Hold the drawing in place with your nondominant hand, and with your dominant hand, use the regular sewing needle to perforate the drawing and note card over the drawn lines. Leave enough space between the holes so the paper and note card don't tear. You need to use the regular needle to perforate the paper because the blunter point of the embroidery needle could cause the papers to crease, crinkle, or tear.

4. Once you poke holes over the entire drawing, remove the paper from the card, but keep it in front of you for reference.

5. Thread the embroidery needle and use it to embroider through the holes in the note card. Make a small knot on the end of your thread so that it stays taut in the first stitch. Be creative, connect dots—there are no limits to the types of stitching that you do. The only consideration you may make is to the weight of your paper. Too much perforation can result in ripping of the card along the dotted line. Don't worry if the back is messy because you can take a second piece of paper or note card and glue it to the inside so that the back of the embroidery work does not show. **[B, C]**

# Gallery

**While having a fully equipped studio, free time, and technical skills are vital to creating your own art and product, they will mean nothing without a little inspiration.** While you can find ideas in the world around you, it is also great to be aware of historical and current art trends and design references to be inspired. Following you will find some of our favorite current working artists and designers.

Margo Wolowiec
*One Day of Status Updates: 9.15.09*
2011
Margo Wolowiec is a San Francisco-based artist who uses weaving as her primary medium. She most often explores communication, particularly our current social media such as Facebook and Twitter, and how it changes dialogue.

Margo Wolowiec
*Conversation No. 1*
2011

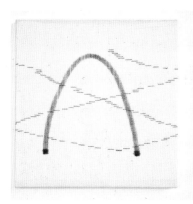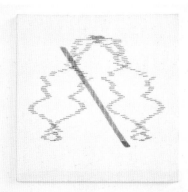

Adrienne Sloane
*Casting Shadows*
2011
The use of textiles and fibers in art can be highly sculptural and also deceive the eye. Textile processes can also be used for nonfiber materials. This piece uses knit wire and cotton, showing a great example of using a nontraditional material.

**RIGHT**
Adrienne Sloane
*Uprooted*
2010
Adrienne Sloane most often uses knitting in unique and creative sculptural ways, defying what we may typically think of as knitting.

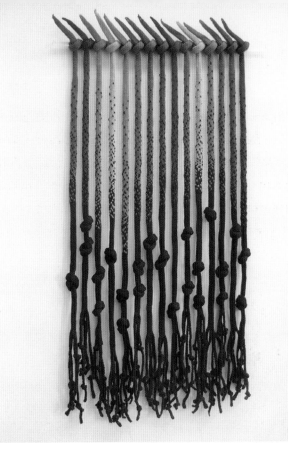

Joetta Maue
*Happily...*
2010
Joetta Maue is an embroidery artist who explores themes of intimacy and family, often using her medium and collage to create three-dimensionality to bring characters and words off the wall. She often uses found objects and repurposes vintage linens and lace on which to embroider.

Erin M Riley
*Loot 2*
2011
Erin M. Riley uses woven tapestry as a main medium, portraying images from our current young-adult culture in the U.S. She often hand-dyes her yarns before weaving the intricate images.

Luke Haynes
*[The American Context #3] American Gothic*
2010
This 90" x 90" (230 x 230 cm) quilt by Luke Haynes is indicative of the rest of his work. Using reclaimed clothes, fabric, batting, and thread, Luke creates highly realistic imagery and narrative through quilting. This piece is in *the Permanent Collection* of the Newark Museum.

**FAR LEFT**
Sabrina Gschwandtner
*Watch + See*
2009
Sabrina Gschwandtner is highly established in the fiber and craft world as an artist, teacher, lecturer, writer, and critic.

**LEFT**
*Watch + See* detail
2009
Sabrina Gschwandtner

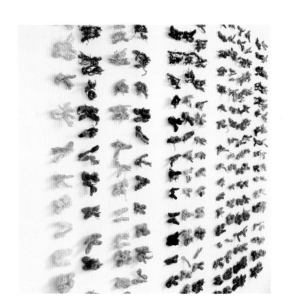

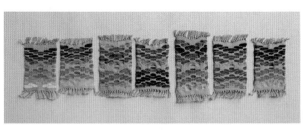

**LEFT**
Tali Weinberg
*Cures for Depressions*
2011
In *Cures for Depressions*, Tali Weinberg created a complete dye reference on the wall using 480 1-inch (2.5 cm) skeins, all naturally dyed. The viewer is able to see the wide variety of colors you can achieve using natural dyes.

**ABOVE**
Tali Weinberg
*Cures for Depressions*
2011
Seven small weavings accompanied the dye reference chart. Each is hand-woven with organic cotton that had been naturally dyed using osage orange, logwood, madder, weld, indigo, and pomegranate.

Photo: Kris Atendido

**FAR LEFT**
Julia Ramsey
*Venetian Collection*
2010
Julia Ramsey is a knitwear designer and fiber artist who uses machine knitting as her main medium. Through clothing, Julia expresses her unique visions for the female body. She views clothing as sculpture, building each piece in a masterful way.

**LEFT**
Julia Ramsey
*Engaged: Tied Up*
2011
This piece was first exhibited at the Textile Arts Center in July, 2011.

**RIGHT**
Stacie Baek
*Untitled 2*
2011
Stacie Baek
Stacie Baek is a recent graduate from MICA who explores her own communication about a specific relationship through text in weaving. Taken from her personal journal, Stacie uses double-weave pick up to spell out intimate, haunting, and often funny statements and thoughts. These pieces are extremely labor-intensive, though small in size.

**FAR RIGHT**
Stacie Baek
*Untitled 3*
2011

**FAR LEFT**
Annie Coggan Crawford
*Grant-MS Loveseat*
2010
An architect by trade, Annie Coggan is fascinated by interior space and the objects put in it. Through embroidery and reworking of found furniture, Coggan creates narrative pieces that are based in history and storytelling, while creating unique products.

**LEFT**
Annie Coggan
*William Faulkner Chair*
2010

**LEFT**
Megan Whitmarsh
*Color Dance Bomb*
2009
Megan Whitmarsh is a working fiber artist who uses fabric and thread as a drawing tool and medium to make soft sculpture. In these pieces, Megan uses embroidery to depict scenes full of life and color.

**BOTTOM LEFT**
Megan Whitmarsh
*Laser Dance Wars*
2009

**RIGHT**
Rachel Rose
*Hand-Painted Silk Shirt*
2011
Through silk painting, Rachel Rose is able to achieve extremely beautiful and painterly designs onto clothing, such as this simple yet elegant T-shirt.

Photo: Kaelen

Photo: Chito Yoshida

**LEFT**
Audrey Louise Reynolds
*Collaboration with Kaelen*
2011
Audrey Louise Reynolds works out of Brooklyn, New York, and is known for her unusual dye techniques. Each short and jacket was dipped in Atlantic ocean salt water, charcoal sumac, with a hint of indigo dye, then wind dried. The shorts were revisited by waves and with two different, shades of Iranian indigo dye. The oceans tide was used here to create wrap around stripes across the legs.

**ABOVE**
Repetto
*Repetto Ballet Flats collaboration*
2011
In collaboration with Repetto, Audrey Louise Reynolds used dye techniques to create unique looks using techniques and natural materials including curry berries, tumeric, and recycled materials.

Katrin Reifeiss
*Hand-dyed shibori*
2011
Katrin Reifiess is a New York-based designer who focuses on dyeing and shibori techniques to create beautiful textiles that become clothing, bags, and other fashion pieces.

**RIGHT**
Emily Fischer, Haptic Lab
*Orcas Islands*
2011
Emily Fischer is an architect by trade, but fell into the world of home goods through quilting. Her beautiful map quilts come in a variety of sizes and can also be custom made for the place you wish to revisit over and over through her pieces.

**BELOW LEFT**
Emily Fischer
*Lower Manhattan detail*
2011

**BELOW RIGHT**
Emily Fischer
*Lower Manhattan quilt*
2011

Caitlin Mociun
**Title:** *Silk Screened Linens*
**Date:** 2011
**Credit:** MOCIUN
**Caption:** Caitlin Mociun is the Brooklyn-based designer behind MOCIUN. A graduate from Rhode Island School of Design, Caitlin is an amazing textile and pattern designer and has recently begun to explore textile design for home goods, as well as custom jewelry that beautifully correspond to her textiles and clothing.

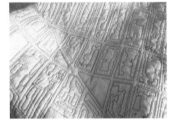

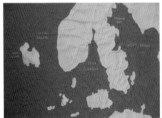

*Photo: Mociun*

**RIGHT**
Erin Considine
*Immrama Collection*
Spring 2011
Erin Considine is a Brooklyn-based
jewelry designer who makes beautiful
naturally dyed and hand-braided
jewelry. She incorporates metal work in
most pieces, creating a nice juxtaposi-
tion between soft and hard.

**BELOW**
Erin Considine
*Immrama Collection*
Spring 2011

Photo: George Barberis

**BELOW, TOP**
Ilana Kohn
*Marbled Jess Shirt*
2011
Ilana Kohn is a small line of clean, easy-
to-wear women's clothing designed and
produced in Brooklyn, New York.

**BELOW**
*Roxey Dress and grey marbled scarf*
2011
Clothing by Ilana Kohn, marbling by
Ilana Kohn + Emily Eibel.

Photo: George Barberis

Photos: Jessica Kaczorowski and Dustin Fenstermacher

**RIGHT, TOP**
Sasha Duerr + Casey Larkin – Adie + George
*Olive Sweater and Dede Skirt*
A/W 2011
Adie + George is made up Sasha Duerr and Casey Larkin, who are both designers, artists, and educators. Through Adie+George, Duerr and Larkin express their love for sustainable design and textiles. Everything is west coast grown, California-spun and -knit natural black and cream alpaca, artisan plant-dyed with "seasonal yellow" (oxalis weeds) and avocado pits.

**RIGHT, BOTTOM**
*Abigail Tunic*
A/W 2011

*Photos: Chloe Aftel*

*Photos: Jonathan Hokklo*

**ABOVE**
KNITTA: Magda Sayeg
*Plan Ahead*
2011
Magda Sayeg is the artist behind Knitta, a group of fiber artists who use their knitting medium to "tag" and "graffiti" public spaces. Shown is a piece in Brooklyn, New York, below the Williamsburg Bridge.

**BELOW**
Jordana Martin, Oak Knit Studio
*Machine knitted and dyed jewelry*
2011
As founder of Oak Knit Studio, Jordana Martin creates machine-knit designs such as these necklaces. Using organic cottons, silks, and cashmere, Jordana makes luxury jewelry that incorporate several textile techniques.

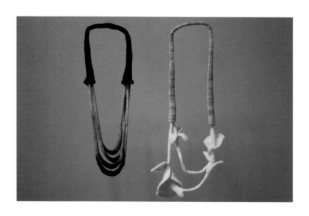

# Resources

## Resource Facilities and Organizations

American Craft Council: *www.craftcouncil.org*

BurdaStyle: *www.burdastyle.com*

Hand Weavers Guild of America: *www.weavespindye.org*

Huddersfield Textile Centre of Excellence:
*www.textilehouse.co.uk*

Natural Dyes International: *www.naturaldyes.org*

Nordic Initiative Clean & Ethical: *www.nicefashion.org*

Open Wear Collaborative Clothing: *www.openwear.org*

Permacouture Institute: *www.permacouture.org*

Source4Style: *www.source4style.com*

Surface Design Association: *www.surfacedesign.org*

Tactile Textile Arts Center: *www.tactilearts.org*

Textile Arts Center: *www.textileartscenter.com*

The Textile Center, Minneapolis:
*www.textilecentermn.org*

Textile Society of America: *www.textilesociety.org*

The Textile Museum, D.C.: *www.textilemuseum.org*

Textile Museum of Canada: *www.textilemuseum.ca*

## Higher Education

California College of the Arts

California State University, Long Beach

Central Saint Martins, UK

Cranbrook Academy of Art

Fashion Institute of Technology

Iowa State University

Kansas State University

Maryland Institute College of Art

Massey University, New Zealand

Nova Scotia College of Art and Design

Ohio State University

Parsons The New School for Design

Philadelphia University

Pratt Institute

Rhode Island School of Design

Royal Academy of Fine Arts, Antwerp

Savannah College of Art and Design

Skidmore College

The Textile Conservation Centre, UK

Tyler School of Art

University College UCC, Denmark

## Books We Love

**Weaving**
*Learning to Weave*
Deborah Chandler
Interweave Press, 2009.

*Sheila Hicks: Weaving as Metaphor*
Nina Stritzler-Levine
Yale University Press, 2006 .

**Printing**
*Printing by Hand*
Lena Corwin
STC Craft, 2008.

**Sewing**
*The BurdaStyle Sewing Handbook*
Nora Abousteit and Alison Kelly
Potter Craft, 2011.

*Vogue Sewing*
Vogue Knitting Magazine
Sixth & Spring Books, 2006.

**Dyeing**
*The Art and Craft of Natural Dyeing*
J. N. Liles
The University of Tennessee Press, 1990.

*A Dyer's Garden: From Plant to Pot, Growing Dyes for Natural Fibers*
Buchanan, Rita
Interweave Press, 1995.

*Dye Plants and Dyeing*
Cannon, John and Margaret
A & C Black, 2003.

*Alabama Stitch Book*
Natalie Chanin
STC Craft, 2008.

*Alabama Studio Style*
Natalie Chanin
STC Craft, 2010.

*Alabama Stitch Design*
Natalie Chanin
STC Craft, 2012.

*Eco Colour*
India Flint
Interweave Press, 2010.

*Hand Dyeing Yarn and Fleece*
Gail Callahan
Storey Publishing, 2010.

*Handweaver's Pattern Directory*
Anne Dixon
Interweave Press, 2007.

*The Handbook of Natural Plant Dyes*
Sasha Duerr
Timber Press, 2011.

*Hoopla*
Leanne Praine
Arsenal Pulp Press, 2011.

*Indigo*
Jenny Baulfour-Paul
Archetype, 2007.

*Koekboya: Natural Dyes and Textiles*
Haral Bohmer
REMHOB-Verlag, 2002.

*Natural Dyes*
Dominique Cardon
Antique Collectors Club Ltd., 2007.

*PUSH: Stitchery*
Jamie Chalmers
Lark Crafts, 2011.

*The Surface Designer's Handbook*
Holly Brackmann
Interweave Press, 2006.

*Synthetic Dyes for Natural Fibers*
Linda Knutson
Interweave Press, 1986.

*Wild Color*
Dean, Jenny
Watson-Guptill Publications, 1999.

## Textile Conservation Resources

*Chemical Principles of Textile Conservation*
Ágnes Tímár-Balázsy and Dinah Eastop
Butterworth-Heinemann, 1998

*Textile Conservator's Manual*
Sheila Landi
Butterworth-Heinemann, 1998

The Textile Museum
www.textilemuseum.org/care/brochures/guidelines.htm

*Unravelling Textiles: A Handbook for the Preservation of Textile Collections*
Foekje Boersma
Archetype Books, 2008

## Textile Blogs We Love

Abigail Doan
www.abigaildoan.blogspot.com

Bobbin Talk
www.bobbintalk.com

BurdaStyle
www.burdastyle.com/blog

Erin Considine
erinconsidine.tumblr.com

Fashion Projects
www.fashionprojects.org

Hand/Eye
handeyemagazine.com

Joetta Maue
littleyellowbirds.blogspot.com

Mr. X Stitch
www.mrxstitch.com

Naturally Dyeing
naturallydyeing.blogspot.com

Pattern Pulp
www.patternpulp.com

Permacouture
permacouturepress.tumblr.com

Poppytalk Handmade
www.poppytalkhandmade.com

Tinctory
tinctory.blogspot.com

World of Textiles
whereinthewot.blogspot.com

## Publications We Love

Fiber Art Now
www.fiberartnow.net

Hand/Eye Magazine
www.handeyemagazine.com

Selvedge Magazine
www.selvedge.org

Surface Design Journal
www.surfacedesign.org

Vogue Knitting
www.vogueknitting.com

## Where to Buy

**Natural Dyes:**
Aurora Silk
www.aurorasilk.com

Botanical Colors
www.botanicalcolors.com

Earthues
www.earthues.com

Kremer Pigments
www.kremerpigments.com

**Synthetic Dyes:**
Dharma Trading Co.
www.dharmatrading.com

Jacquard
www.jacquardproducts.com

ProChem
www.prochem.com

**Weaving Supplies:**
Schacht Spindle Co
www.schachtspindle.com

Textile Arts Center
www.shoptextileartscenter.com

**Yarns for Knitting, Crochet, and Weaving:**
Brooklyn General
www.brooklyngeneral.com

Brooklyn Tweed
www.brooklyntweed.net/yarn

Lion Brand
www.lionbrand.com

Purl Soho
www.purlsoho.com

WEBS
www.yarn.com

**Machine Knitting:**
Peter Patchis
www. peterpatchisyarns.com

**Sewing Supplies:**
Dharma Trading Co
www.dharmatrading.com

Jo-Ann Fabrics
www.joann.com

Singer
www.singerco.com

**Screen Printing Supplies:**
Standard Screen Supply
www.standardscreen.com

Victory Screen Supply
www.victoryfactory.com

# About the Authors

**Visnja Popovic** moved to the U.S. from Belgrade, Serbia, in 1991. She studied textiles at the Rhode Island School of Design, including a semester studying traditional batik dyeing and woodblock printing in Accra, Ghana. After graduating, Visnja moved to New York City to work in the surface design industry. In 2007, she returned to school to receive a masters in Art Education from Pratt Institute. Since then, she has taught textile design and weaving in New York City and South Africa. In 2009, Visnja co-founded the Textile Arts Center, LLC; an educational institution that specializes in supporting the textile community and advocates conserving traditional techniques. Visnja's specialty is weaving. She lives in Brooklyn, New York.

Born and raised in Brooklyn, **Owyn Ruck** had the luxury of growing up in a creative and artistic environment. She graduated from Skidmore College with a B.S. in Fine Art, with a concentration in fibers and printmaking. After several years of exploring the interior design industry, Owyn met Visnja and together they founded the Textile Arts Center. While she knows and loves many textile media, Owyn's first love is arts education, providing others with a creative outlet and the opportunity to learn. Owyn lives in Brooklyn, New York.

**Visnja** And **Owyn** would like to thank
Isa Rodrigues, Addison Walz, Pauline Shapiro,
Alexandra Labriola, and Jordana Martin

# Index